WOODWORKING
JOINERY
by Hand

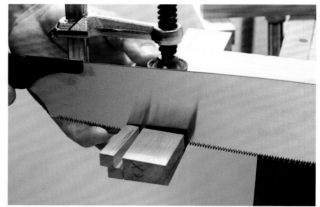

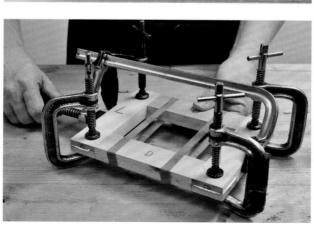

WOODWORKING JOINERY
by Hand

Innovative techniques using Japanese saws and jigs

TOYOHISA SUGITA

THE GUILD OF MASTER CRAFTSMAN PUBLICATIONS

CONTENTS

CHAPTER 1: BASIC TOOLS

Introduction 6
What is a ripping guide? 12
What is a cross-cut guide? 21
Length hook: making cuts with the same dimensions 25
Hand saws 27
Other essential tools 36

CHAPTER 2: FRAMING

Level 1 42
Half lap joint
photo frame

Level 2 52
Rabbeted half lap joint
photo frame

Level 3 61
Splined mitre joint
photo frame

Level 4 71
Mitred half lap joint
photo frame

Level 5 78
Mitred half lap joint with
groove or rabbeted frame

Level 6 87
Bridle joint frame

Level 7 92
Grooved bridle joint frame
(mitred inset panel)

CHAPTER 3: MAKING BOXES

Level 1
Rabbet joint box — 100

Level 2
Case mitre joint box — 105

Level 3
Box joint basics:
five interlocking pins — 116

Level 4
Box joint that hides
bottom board rabbets — 126

Level 5
Rabbet joint box — 131

Level 6
Finger-jointed box
with lid — 138

Level 7
Frame and panel
joint box — 147

Level 8
Drawers — 153

CHAPTER 4: GUIDES AND JIGS

Shooting board and bench hook	162
Mitre cutting guide with T-shaped stopper	172
Rabbeting guide	186
Self-aligning groove cutting guide/Accurate Guide	193
Case mitre cutting guide	220
Mortice and tenon joint	230
Gluing planks together and homemade clamps	239
Saw guide for set-saw blade	242
Tail guide and saw blade spacer with bevel	244
Tapered sliding dovetail joint	251

Suppliers	275
Metric to imperial conversion table	276
About the author	277
Index	278

INTRODUCTION

The woodworking methods in this book can turn complete beginners into master woodworkers. The innovative 'Sugita woodworking method' uses hand-sawing jigs, some with magnets, to help beginners make straight and right-angle cuts. Along with a description of the basic tools you will need, this book shows you clever techniques to work expertly with joints without using screws or nails, like a seasoned woodworker.

THE BENEFITS OF USING HAND TOOLS

If you want to enjoy peaceful woodworking, hand tools (like hand saws, planes, etc.) are much better than power tools. Many of us prefer not to use power tools if possible due to noise, safety and workspace limitations. However, it is much more difficult to make straight and right-angle cuts with hand saws. Perfectly straight cuts are always challenging for non-professional woodworkers, and this is where the unique methods featured in this book come in.

As woodworking hobbyists, we can't always work wood as much as we would like to, so it is no surprise that we don't have the same level of skills as true craftspeople. Neither do we always have the special jigs and tools needed for a specific product. Finishing our projects quickly is also not a priority as there is no deadline, so we can produce our work slowly and carefully. We dream of making a work of art that has no gaps in the joints, even if the techniques used aren't very advanced.

So, how can I learn to make advanced projects like a true craftsperson with only hand tools? In the past, the answer would probably have been, 'Practise, practise, practise.' That is still true, but what I'd like to tell you is that you don't need to be specially trained. We have the unique methods you'll need explained in this book. In the table below, you can see that, using these methods, hand tools can achieve the same high machining accuracy of power tools.

	MACHINING ACCURACY	NOISE	SAFETY
POWER TOOL WOODWORKING	✓	✗	✗
HAND TOOL WOODWORKING	✗	✓	✓
METHODS USED IN THIS BOOK	✓	✓	✓

THE STORY BEHIND THE SUGITA WOODWORKING METHOD

I used to be a staunch power tool guy and the market is full of excellent tools. So, I bought some tools by mail order and made my own table and drill press. These tools proved very useful when making beds, cabinets and chairs for my children. One day, I realised that noise from power tools is a big problem for woodworkers in apartment complexes and finding a solution to that problem soon became my 'homework'.

In the beginning, I was so focused on how to keep noise levels low that I didn't even consider using hand tools. There were times when I seriously thought about using power tools in a soundproofed chamber or using a vacuum cleaner to collect sawdust. Still, I couldn't get rid of the problems, so I built a tent in my room and worked in that. But no matter how much I thought about it, I couldn't solve the problem. I was out of ideas.

In the end, I was forced to steer towards purely hand tool woodworking. Even so, I thought there was no way I could cut straight or at right angles with a handsaw. In my quest to figure out how to make things 'straight and right angled', I came up with a method of horizontal ripping using a guide with a magnetic sheet attached. I had seen right angle and 45-degree cross-cutting methods elsewhere, but my question was how to perform the ripping. In particular, how to position and cut perpendicularly into the end grain. The problem is that wood joinery is a combination of these cross and rip cuts. If this isn't resolved, we can't move forward. After much trial and error, I arrived at my current unique method of attaching spacers to the vertical ripping guide using magnetic sheets.

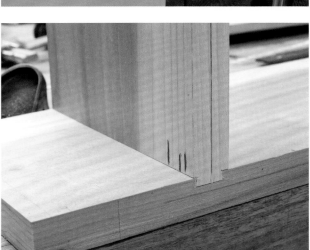

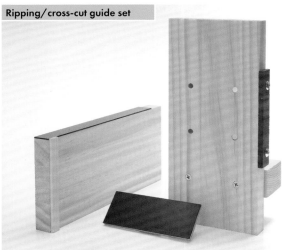

Ripping/cross-cut guide set

Further evolution

Once the decision was made to use two basic guides, one for vertical ripping and one for horizontal cross-cutting, a rule was soon born: **'If you can see the area marked with an O, insert a saw blade spacer'**. This rule came about because, when sawing, the thickness of the saw blade is lost in the form of sawdust.

In woodworking, it's important to take this fact into account and decide which side of the marked line you wish to cut. The same is true for the unique methods in this book. However, I found that I could use the thickness of the saw blade I was employing in a specific manner. This allows us to control which side of the marked line to cut into. I found that I could cut very accurately because I didn't have to rely on visual measurements as I did in the past.

This idea led to the discovery of a technical theory called 'one-shot cutting'. This eliminates the need to adjust the fit with chisels and planers after everything has been processed. Another useful discovery was the 'depth stop'. When affixed to a saw blade it helps with both the cutting and with controlling the depth of the cut. In particular, it prevents over or under cutting when using visual measurements. I have found that these rules and methods are much more efficient, as they eliminate the need for excessively marking up the wood.

Toyohisa Sugita

MEASUREMENTS

All the dimensions in this book are expressed in millimetres (mm). **R** represents radius, **t** represents thickness and both **Ø** and **D** represent diameter. Screw sizing is listed as: 'M4 x 15 plate', which means a countersunk head screw with a thickness of 4mm and a length of 15mm.

HAND PLANES

If you don't have the necessary hand plane, you can use a sanding block instead.

NOTE ON SAWS

In this book, I have used a type of flush-cut saw called the MIRAI 265, which is ideal for the special methods used here. You can also use other straight-toothed Japanese flush-cut saws (see page 275 for suppliers list). However, please note that every flush-cut saw has its own characteristics and may not match what is shown in this book exactly so make sure you try out the saw you choose carefully.

Chapter 1
BASIC TOOLS

This chapter introduces various basic tools, including hand saw guides developed for the special woodworking methods in this book, and shows you how to make and use them. The most frequently used saw in this book is a flush-cut Japanese saw.

Below: left to right, Cross-cut guide, spacer with magnetic strip and commercially available ripping guide.

WHAT IS A RIPPING GUIDE?

A ripping guide is used to make cuts that run parallel to the grain. By attaching spacers of different thicknesses, you can position the saw to cut into the wood at the exact position you want, while still running parallel to the ripping guide. The unique methods used in this book have a specific rule when using a ripping guide: '**If you can see the area marked with an O, insert a spacer**.' This will be explained later in further detail, but for now, keep this rule in mind.

PROCESSING WOOD WITH A RIPPING GUIDE

Joints between two pieces of wood are made by cutting along, or against, the grain of your wood and then cutting off any unnecessary material. The ripping guide is specifically used to cut wood along the woodgrain. Note that the figures on the right also show cross-cuts. We will use a cross-cut guide – introduced later in this section – for those particular cuts.

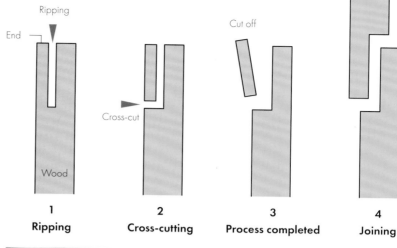

1
Ripping

2
Cross-cutting

3
Process completed

4
Joining

1 Attach some thin, detachable double-sided tape to the spacer in three places – centre, left and right. Let the edge of the tape stick up a few millimetres above the top of the ripping guide so you can easily peel it off with your fingers.

2 Place the clamp just slightly below the target cut depth. To maintain stability, do not clamp too far down.

3 Touch the saw blade to the magnetic sheet and make a straight cut into the wood.

Clamp the ripping guide to the workbench. Take a spacer of the appropriate thickness and attach it to the ripping guide with double-sided tape. The thickness of the spacer determines where you will cut into the wood, so choose carefully. The magnetic sheet attached to the spacer stabilizes your saw blade and allows you to cut in a controlled manner. This method can be used to make both straight and right-angle cuts.

HOW TO USE A RIPPING GUIDE

1 This photo shows a dry fit, half lap joint. It hasn't been glued or sanded. The vertical piece (leftmost) is called the 'stile'. The horizontal piece on the right is called the 'rail'. The letter 'F' represents the front sides of each piece. With the unique methods used in this book, there is no need to mark lines on the wood and there is almost no correction needed – you can do high-precision fitting in a single cut. Follow each step to see how.

SAWDUST CATCHER

Catch sawdust from your work by fitting a simple plastic resealable bag beneath your ripping guide.

1 First, fold a corrugated plastic sheet in half and insert it into the bag – the sheet will force open the bag because it wants to return to its original shape.

2 Now attach the open bag to the underside of your ripping guide using double-sided tape. During sawing, most of your sawdust will fall comfortably into the open bag.

Mark for ripping

2 Clamp the lumber under a spacer and mark along the spacer edge. You don't need to mark lines with this method, but this demonstrates in this step where the wood will be cut.

3 Make it a habit to put an O on necessary parts and an X on any unnecessary parts before cutting. The O and X are opposite each other in this case since we are making a half lap joint. In woodworking, the saw should *always* be placed on the side marked with an X. This is to ensure that the thickness of the O marked area remains accurate.

4 Clamp the rail in the jig, making sure you clamp both rails and stiles to the ripping guide so that the front side (marked 'F') is always visible. Also, make sure that you can always see the X mark on the end, in front of the spacer.

5 The photo shows wood that has been cut vertically to the right depth. Here, it is key to understand that the saw blade has a certain thickness. When you cut a piece of wood, this blade's thickness is also removed from the target piece. This is called the **kerf**. In this example, the kerf is within the X marked area in front of the marked line.

6 Next, clamp the stile in the jig with the 'F' facing forwards. The O mark should be visible. In the previous step, the X mark was visible here. Now, if you saw along the marked line, the kerf occurs inside the area marked with width O. Be warned, this will make the piece too thin! If this happens, when the rail and stile are fitted together, there will be a gap equivalent to the saw blade's thickness of the saw blade and the project will fail.

7 To solve this problem, **place a saw blade that is the same thickness as the one you are using behind the stile**. Then, clamp them together. Now, the stile has been pushed forwards to the width of the kerf. In the photo, you can see that this same-sized saw blade has been placed between the ripping guide and the stile so that the marked line is visible slightly ahead of the spacer edge.

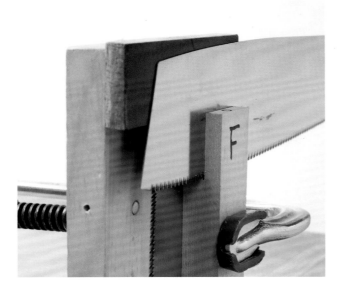

8 If you use this method, the kerf will always be inside the X marked area and your project will not have a gap. This goes back to the rule for this book's unique methods: '**Insert a saw blade as a spacer when the area marked with an O is visible in front of the spacer**'. It is a very important rule!

9 Using this rule, you can saw accurate joints with a single cut. It also means that the time-consuming work of gradually cutting and adjusting the parts with a hand plane or chisel is almost eliminated. It's a great feature of the methods used in this book.

BUILDING A RIPPING/CROSS-CUT GUIDE

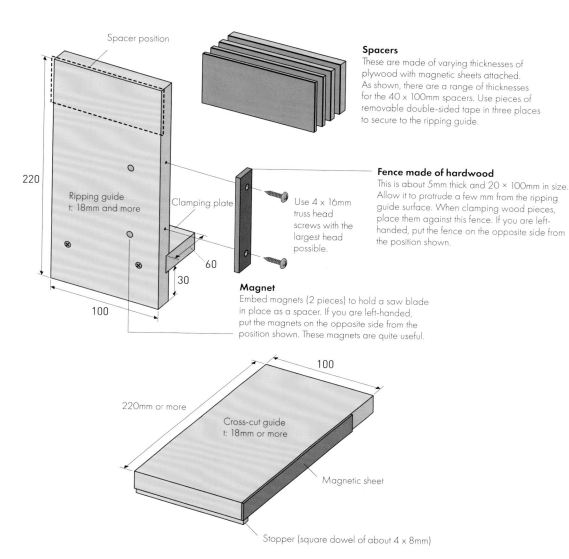

Spacer position

220

Ripping guide
t: 18mm and more

100

Clamping plate

30

60

Spacers
These are made of varying thicknesses of plywood with magnetic sheets attached. As shown, there are a range of thicknesses for the 40 x 100mm spacers. Use pieces of removable double-sided tape in three places to secure to the ripping guide.

Fence made of hardwood
This is about 5mm thick and 20 × 100mm in size. Allow it to protrude a few mm from the ripping guide surface. When clamping wood pieces, place them against this fence. If you are left-handed, put the fence on the opposite side from the position shown.

Use 4 x 16mm truss head screws with the largest head possible.

Magnet
Embed magnets (2 pieces) to hold a saw blade in place as a spacer. If you are left-handed, put the magnets on the opposite side from the position shown. These magnets are quite useful.

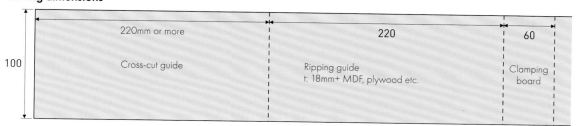

100

220mm or more

Cross-cut guide
t: 18mm or more

Magnetic sheet

Stopper (square dowel of about 4 x 8mm)

Cutting dimensions

100

220mm or more	220	60
Cross-cut guide	Ripping guide t: 18mm+ MDF, plywood etc.	Clamping board

Required materials

- 18mm+ MDF, plywood etc.
- Hardwood (for the fence)
- Double-sided tape

- Magnetic sheeting
- Magnets (2 pcs.)
- 4 x 8mm square dowel

- Plywood of various thicknesses (for spacers)
- 4 x 16mm truss head screws (2 pcs.)

OTHER TYPES OF RIPPING GUIDES

Rabbet guide

This is a ripping/cross-cut guide for wide material (wood). Attach spacers of different thicknesses to the guide, determine the cutting position of the material and make vertical/horizontal cuts.

If the material is wider than the guide, just shift the piece to the middle of the guide, re-clamp and then cut the rest of the material. See page 193 for details.

New-type ripping guide

Spacer plates cut from acrylic sheets

Mortice-and-tenon joint

This type of guide uses spacers, ranging from 0.1mm to 10mm in thickness, to set the exact position for making precise cuts.

As an example, when creating a mortice-and-tenon joint, mortices can first be drilled and then this guide can be used to make a tenon of the appropriate thickness. The diagrams opposite show how it is assembled.

New-type ripping guide: 3-dimensional view

Components

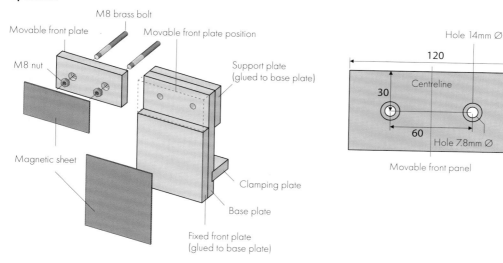

- M8 brass bolt
- Movable front plate
- Movable front plate position
- M8 nut
- Support plate (glued to base plate)
- Magnetic sheet
- Clamping plate
- Base plate
- Fixed front plate (glued to base plate)

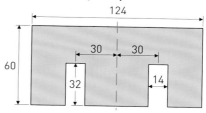

Hole 14mm Ø
120
18
Centreline
30
8
60
60
Hole 7.8mm Ø
Movable front panel

Modifications for star grip knob

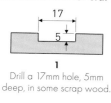

1
Drill a 17mm hole, 5mm deep, in some scrap wood.

17
5

2
Flip the star grip knob (orange) upside down and insert in hole.

Enlarge the hole in the star grip knob body.

3
Drill an 8.5mm hole.

8.5

8.5

Widen the hole with an 8.5mm drill bit.

Dimensions of spacer plate

124
30   30
60
32   14

This is a dimensional drawing of the spacer plate. This plate is used when cutting out the spacer with a trim router or router. Use a 12mm flush trim bit with a bearing. MDF or plywood with a thickness of about 9–12mm is best.

Modifications for star grip knob

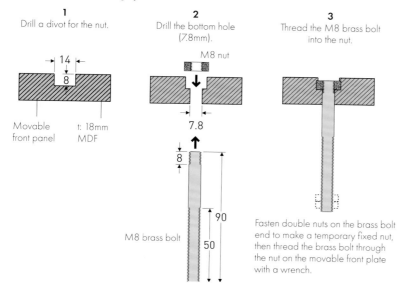

1
Drill a divot for the nut.

14
8
Movable front panel
t: 18mm MDF

2
Drill the bottom hole (7.8mm).

M8 nut
7.8
8
90
50
M8 brass bolt

3
Thread the M8 brass bolt into the nut.

Fasten double nuts on the brass bolt end to make a temporary fixed nut, then thread the brass bolt through the nut on the movable front plate with a wrench.

New-type ripping guide dimensions

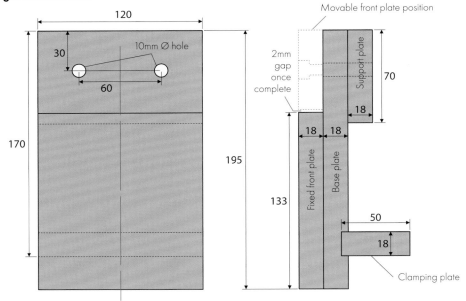

Spacer dimensions

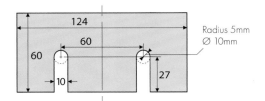

If the material is too thick to rout out the U-shape seen, you can simply drill a 10mm Ø hole (dotted line) instead. (For thin spacers, use scissors to cut out the U-shape.)

Cutting dimensions

60	195	70	133	50
Movable front panel	Base plate	Support plate (70mm)	Fixed front panel	Clamping plate

120

t: 18mm MDF

Unit: mm
t: thickness
Ø: diameter

ALUMINIUM RIPPING GUIDE

This product, shown for reference, has magnets embedded in its face to hold a saw blade, which is used as an additional spacer. It can be altered for right-handed or left-handed users by changing attachment positions. In addition, it can be turned into a new-type ripping guide by adding optional parts.

WHAT IS A CROSS-CUT GUIDE?

A cross-cut guide is used when cutting across the grain of a piece of wood. Simply place the material against this guide to make a right-angle cut. Using the length hook, introduced later in this section, you can make the exact same length cut repeatedly. Commercial aluminium cross-cut guides can also make 45-degree cuts.

MAKING A CROSS-CUT GUIDE

1 Attach a magnetic sheet to the body of the guide. While holding a square along the side where the sheet is attached, use glue to fix a small piece of wood to the short edge as a 'hook'. The hook and magnet allow you to make consistent right-angle cuts.

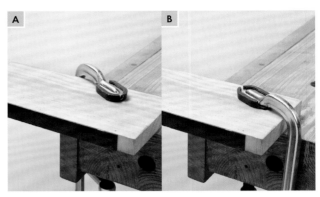

2 As shown, there are two ways to clamp the cross-cut guide to a workbench. Either method is fine, but for case B, be sure to clamp the guide so that it won't interfere with the saw.

3 When clamping the target piece of wood, be sure to pull it firmly against the hook. Also, position the clamp at the half-width point of the material to be cut.

4 Place your blade directly against the magnetic sheet and saw straight down. At first, you may find it difficult to handle the clamps. Practise clamping different sizes of material to make sure you can clamp things properly.

5 From below, you can see that I am pinching the material with my left index finger and thumb. Pull the material in the direction of the arrow to ensure that it rests firmly against the hook. If you don't do this, the cut might not be right-angled.

6 Hold the material with your index finger and then push the bottom jaw of the clamp up with the three remaining fingers.

7 Lower the top jaw of the clamp while holding the material firmly in place.

8 Place the saw blade against the magnetic sheet. Be sure to saw straight down.

9 When cutting wide pieces, place the cross-cut guide on top of the piece and clamp the guide, piece and table together.

10 Here is a commercially available cross-cut guide made of aluminium.

11 The aluminium cross-cut guide comes with two screws. These can be used to fasten the guide at an angle to make 45-degree cuts for photo frames and other products.

12 The photo above shows the guide, with screws installed, making a 45-degree cut.

13 The cross-cut guide can be used in other useful ways, including turning it upside down to cut different angles.

14 You can glue wooden craft sticks on the aluminium cross-cut guide to make temporary hooks. This can help you cut different materials at identical angles.

15 This photo shows a cut being made with the temporary hooks in place.

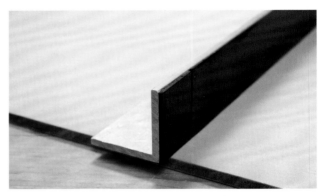

16 This is a piece of 30 × 30 × 3mm aluminium right-angle material. Even though this is normally for making long cuts, it can be used as a cross-cut guide by attaching a magnetic sheet to one side and securing it to the target piece with a clamp or double-sided tape. Replace the magnetic sheets mentioned in this section whenever they become too scratched up.

CUT-OFF CAPTURE TRAY

To capture cut-offs when cross-cutting, you can attach paper plates to an arm that projects from under the workbench.

1 Using a strip of hook-and-loop fastener attached to the bottom of the paper plate, attach it to the arm under your workbench.

2 If you stack two paper plates, one on top of the other, you can easily pick up the top one and throw away the cut-offs, instead of struggling to undo the hook-and-loop fastener strip to remove the bottom plate from the arm.

LENGTH HOOK: MAKING CUTS WITH THE SAME DIMENSIONS

The length hook is very useful if you want to cut pieces to the same dimension and it can also be used to process rabbets and mortice-and-tenon joints.

1 This section introduces a very important woodworking technique: cutting wood to the same dimensions. First, mark the length you want to cut. Starting from the left end will make the next step easier.

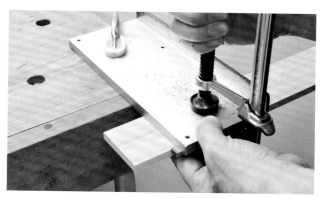

2 Align your mark with the edge of the magnetic sheet on the cross-cut guide and clamp together. Using this book's unique method, the portion of wood that is under the cross-cut guide is the desired length of cut. The part that sticks out from the magnetic sheet, to the right, is excess.

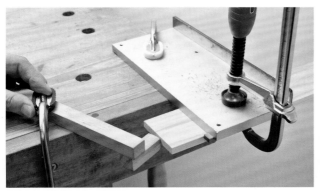

3 Place the length hook against the end of the material and clamp it securely to the workbench.

4 Once the length hook is secure, loosen the clamp holding the material. Make sure the material end butts up to the hook. This step is a precaution in case there is a gap between the material and the length hook when you tightened everything down.

5 Saw off the piece.

6 Remove the clamp. Take out the material cut to the required size. Place the remaining material (excess) against the length hook, clamp it and saw again. This way the material can be cut to the same size with high precision.

7 When making short cuts, tuck the length hook under the cross-cut guide and place it against the end of the material.

8 When making even shorter cuts, the length hook will not be able to reach the material. Instead, use a block of scrap wood as a length hook by directly attaching it to the underside of the cross-cut guide with double-sided tape.

HAND SAWS

We recommend using straight-toothed blades for most of the methods described in this book, mostly because they improve precision. In addition, straight-toothed blades don't scratch the magnetic sheets on the guides as much as other types of blades. When using, the blade sometimes gets caught in the wood, which makes it difficult to continue. Despite this, we still recommend this type. The solution for difficult sawing is described on page 28. Please make sure you have two blades available.

Straight-toothed replacement blade

Blade length: 265mm

Pitch: 1.75mm

Thickness: 0.60mm

Kerf: 0.60mm

About the handle

You can use a pistol grip or straight handle for your saw. For normal use, the pistol grip is easier. Don't grip too firmly, and hold the saw loosely. The fingers will hook nicely at the end of the grip and won't slip. You'll also find that the angle of the wrist and elbow when cutting is more natural with the pistol grip saw. On the other hand, straight handles allow you to keep the saw flat when cutting wide or long pieces of wood. We use both types of handle based on need.

HOW TO USE A SAW WITH A MAGNETIC GUIDE

This is a little different from normal sawing and the secret is to keep the blade horizontal to the wood. Here we need to angle the blade down and saw as close to horizontal as possible. Make sure the width of the saw guide (the magnetic sheet) is less than 30mm.

Wood
Magnetic sheet

Saw guide
Wood

By laying the saw down, the entire blade is positioned within the length of the magnetic sheet. This increases stability and prevents the sheet's surface from being scratched by the teeth.

The rear end of the saw blade is sticking out because the blade is at an angle. This causes a lack of stability. Also, in this position the magnetic sheet will be easily scratched.

Tang
Saw guide
Wood

Pistol grip
Saw guide
Wood

When cutting wide pieces of wood, use a straight-handled saw. It helps keep the blade flat and this increases stability. Begin sawing, as shown, from the centre of the saw blade and pull to the tip. Gradually move on to use the entire blade.

If you use a pistol grip for this type of cut, the heel will hit the wood and you won't be able to lay the saw down properly (see the dotted circle). In addition, the blade will stick out from the magnetic sheet and make the saw unstable, scratching the magnetic sheet.

TROUBLESHOOTING

If the saw blade gets stuck, gently press down with your finger or thumb on the section to be cut off. By doing this, the kerf can spread out in a V-shape, which helps the saw pass more smoothly.

You can also try coating the saw blade with candle wax (be careful as it may clog up), or try spraying it with a tiny bit of silicone spray.

TYPES OF HAND SAW

To follow the tutorials in this book you will need a straight-toothed, flush-cut Japanese saw with non-set teeth so that the handmade guides in the book will not be scratched.

Set-tooth saws: Most saws have set teeth. The saw blade is set alternately on the left and right side. This reduces friction between the blade and the cut edge of the wood, making it easier to eject wood chips. The resulting cut will be larger and may bend, making accurate wood assembly impossible.

Non-set tooth/flush-cut saws: The saw blade does not protrude outwards and cuts straight into the wood, accurately, and with less waste. It does not scratch the object.

1 Straight handle.

2 and **3** Flush-cut, straight-toothed Japanese saws with pistol grip (saw blade thickness: 0.6mm).

4 Flush-cut, straight-toothed Japanese saw with pistol grip (saw blade thickness: 0.4mm).

5 Japanese coping saw. The blade should be mounted to cut when pulling and the angle should be variable, meaning you can cut sideways as well as straight down. A strong blade that can withstand heavy use is recommended.

REPLACEMENT BLADES

Normally, dull replacement blades are thrown out, but for these techniques you can reuse them as spacers. There are a surprisingly large number of people who are obsessed with sharpening their planer blades and chisels, but don't consider the sharpness of their saws as being important. If the blade is dull, it will slip and it will be difficult to make precise cuts.

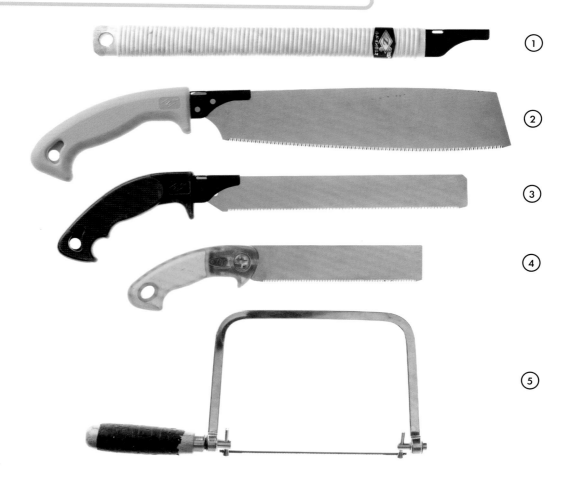

Prevent burrs and chips

Burrs will often appear at the end of your cuts, as shown. To prevent this, start cutting with the saw blade in a horizontal position. Then, when you are close to the end of the cut, lower the saw blade slightly to cut the end part first, then return it to horizontal and cut the rest. When lowering the hand of the saw blade, make sure that the tip of the saw blade does not protrude from the magnetic sheet of the cross-cut guide.

Setting the cut depth

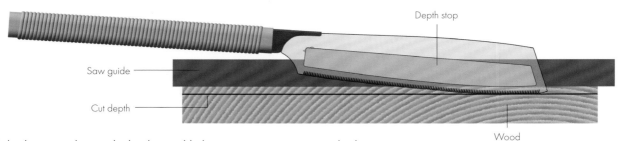

Depth stop

Saw guide

Cut depth

Wood

A depth stop can be attached to the saw blade to maintain a constant cut depth.
These stops can be quite effective in certain situations, like when creating rabbet joints.

 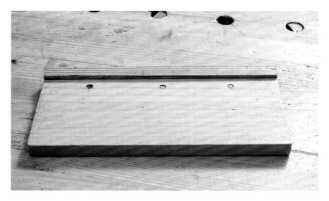

1 This photo shows a custom-made brass stopper. This particular type of stopper has a secondary benefit: it makes the saw blade heavier, which creates a downwards force – and this makes it easier to cut. You can also use something like wood craft sticks to make your depth stops.

2 You can make your own depth-stop setting guide, as shown, for quicker set ups. Magnets are embedded in the guide so that the blade is held in place when butted up against the hook.

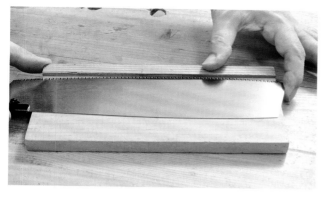

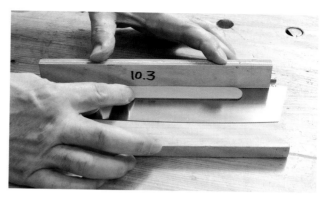

3 To use, place a Japanese flush-cut saw blade on magnets and push the back of the blade up against the hook. If your saw has a curved blade, be sure to carefully even out the spaces caused by the bends on each end.

4 Hold a small block of wood of the proper depth against the hook to act as a spacer. Then, use double-sided tape to attach a thin stir stick – or something similar – to act as a depth stop. The width of the spacer in the photo is 10.3mm, so the depth of cut will also be 10.3mm. Another way to make a depth stop is to mark the depth of the desired cut on the saw blade with a marker and then attach the stir stick.

CUT OFF OLD SAW BLADE 'TOE' AND USE

Cutting off the toe of a saw blade with tin snips can be useful if you need to start cutting in the middle of a piece of wood.

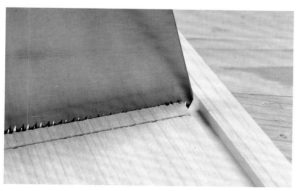

This photo shows the second cut of a housing joint. Cutting the toe off the saw allows us to begin cutting *inside the groove* that has already been made (the tip is inside the groove in the photo). This allows us to make T-shaped grooves.

HOW TO HOLD AND CUT WITH A HAND SAW

1 Hold the handle softly and cut with the blade resting against the magnetic sheet. The end of the grip is hooked, so it won't slip out of your hand even if gripped loosely. If you hold the saw blade too tightly, it won't remain on the magnetic sheet during cutting. To soften your grip, you can place your index finger on top of the handle.

2 Grip softly when using the ripping guide to cut into the end of a block. Place your forefinger almost directly on top of the handle to help apply a slight downwards force on the blade. Apply less force than you think you need!

Posture when sawing

3 To saw straight, the operator's elbow should be an extension of the saw blade. Stand at a slight angle, rather than directly facing the wood (see step 6 on page 33).

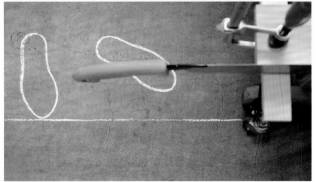

4 These photos show the position of the feet. The white line on the floor is parallel to the magnetic sheet on the guide (i.e. it represents an extension of the saw).

5 If you stand directly in front of the wood when you saw, your elbow will hit your body and the blade will bend. To prevent this, make sure that your feet do not cross the white line marked out in the previous step.

6 To get used to this sawing method, first try to keep your right eye directly above the saw blade (if you are right-handed). Your elbow should be positioned so that it is an extension of the saw blade.

7 To check whether the saw blade is moving in a straight line, attach a metal rod – with a magnetic sheet stuck to it, as shown – to the saw blade. You will hear the metal rod peeling off or sticking back onto the blade if it bends. This method also has the unexpected effect of adding weight to the saw blade, which makes it easier to cut the wood. Here we are using a 220 × 15 × 3mm square brass bar.

8 The depth stop introduced previously was invented when I took the idea of using a metal rod's weight to make cutting easier just a step further. A 4mm-thick brass plate was used.

WHEN STARTING OUT

Choose the straightest wood possible

1 Measure with calipers and choose wood that is as uniform in thickness and width as possible.

Mark out a datum line

2 When cutting long pieces of wood to the desired dimensions, always try to mark the straightest edge with a line. This is called a datum line. Any right-angle lines can be marked by placing a square on the datum line. When cutting, hold the reference line against the hook on the cross-cut guide as often as possible. It's not common practice to mark right-angle lines on the opposite edge from the datum line with a square. For example, in box making, the wood should always be cut with the datum line on the bottom of the box.

Cutting ends

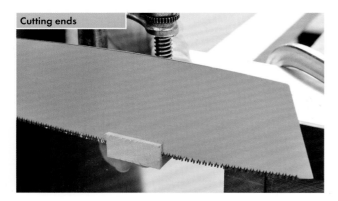

3 First things first, be sure to cut off the ends of your wood. When wood is stored, pebbles may embed in the ends, so it's best to cut off a few millimetres to prevent damage to your tools. This is also done to make sure the ends are at right angles.

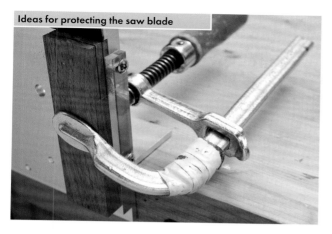
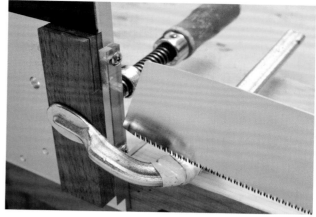

4 When cutting with a ripping guide, the saw may derail due to excessive momentum. This will cause the blade to hit the clamp and bend the teeth. To prevent such accidents, be sure to tape a rubber sheet around the clamp.

Marking and cutting

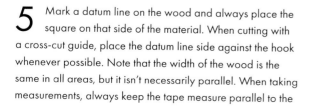

5 Mark a datum line on the wood and always place the square on that side of the material. When cutting with a cross-cut guide, place the datum line side against the hook whenever possible. Note that the width of the wood is the same in all areas, but it isn't necessarily parallel. When taking measurements, always keep the tape measure parallel to the edge of the wood and make a habit of always starting from its left side. It's best to transfer the material directly to the cross-cut guide (without flipping or turning) so that the area under the guide is exactly where it needs to be. Even if you are left-handed, these are good rules of thumb (see steps 1 and 2 on page 22).

OTHER ESSENTIAL TOOLS

Here are some of the excellent tools I use regularly. See page 275 for suppliers. The most important angles in woodworking are the right angle and 45-degree angle. Right angles are particularly important. Choose a high-precision square or a carpenter's square.

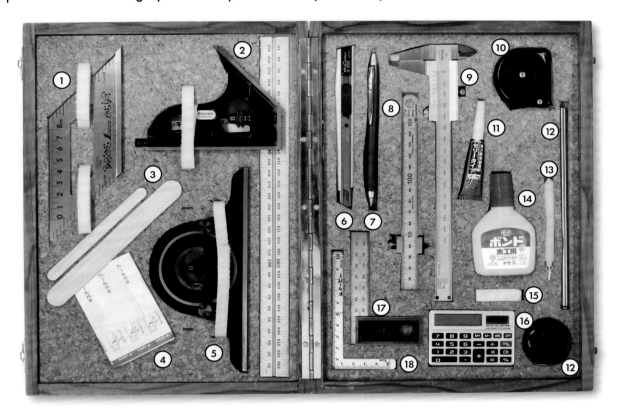

1 Speed square: helps make 45-degree and 135-degree angles.

2 Combination square: the right-angled part moves over the object.

3 Craft sticks: attach to saw blade to control cut depth. Sometimes used as a positioning hook.

4 Bandages: for first-aid purposes.

5 Protractor: attached to a combination square to measure angles.

6 Utility knife/box cutter.

7 Pencil.

8 Ruler with ruler stop: used to mark specific distances from the edge of your material, or to set up your marking gauge.

9 Calipers: used for measuring the thickness, diameter, internal diameter and depth of materials with an accuracy of $5/100$ of a millimetre.

10 Measuring tape: there is a hook at the end of the tape for hooking onto an object or pushing against an object to measure its length.

11 Instant glue.

12 Marking gauge: reassemble for use.

13 Candle: for applying wax onto saw blades.

14 Adhesive (woodworking glue).

15 Rubber.

16 Calculator.

17 Adjustable square: loosening the centre screw moving the jig creates an L-shaped square or a T-shaped square.

18 Square: use different sizes of square for different purposes.

Calipers

Excellent for measuring the thickness, diameter, internal diameter and depth of wood to an accuracy of 5/100 of a millimetre. It is mainly used in this book to measure the thickness of a saw blade and various spacers.

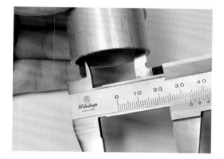

Measuring inside diameter.

Measuring thickness and width.

Measuring depth (insert depth rod).

How to use calipers

The figure shows a caliper holding a round object and measuring its diameter. Calipers have two scales: a main scale, written on the body; and a vernier scale, which slides.

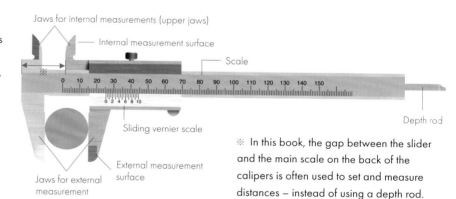

Jaws for internal measurements (upper jaws)

Internal measurement surface

Scale

Sliding vernier scale

Depth rod

Jaws for external measurement

External measurement surface

※ In this book, the gap between the slider and the main scale on the back of the calipers is often used to set and measure distances – instead of using a depth rod.

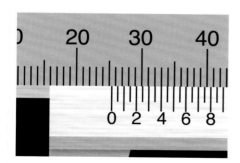

This is an enlarged view of the main scale and vernier scale. First, look at where the zero on the lower vernier scale is located on the main scale. Here, the measurement is between 25mm and 26mm. This tells us that the diameter is roughly in the 25–26mm range. Next, find where the main scale and vernier scale overlap in a perfectly straight line.

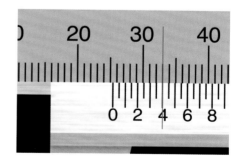

In this figure, the red line overlap is straight. This is position 4 on the vernier scale, so our reading becomes 25.4mm. Precise measurements such as this are one of the great benefits of these types of calipers.

Frequently used technique when hand sawing

1 This technique is easier than depth rod measuring for gaps. Place the tip of the calipers on the piece and lower the outer upper jaw of the vernier scale as shown (see arrow).

2 This is the view from the back. The outer upper jaw is touching the wood. Now we just need to read the measurement on the front of the calipers.

Tools for stabilizing/clamps

Clamps are indispensable for fastening and securing materials when gluing.
You can never have enough clamps! See page 275 for suppliers.

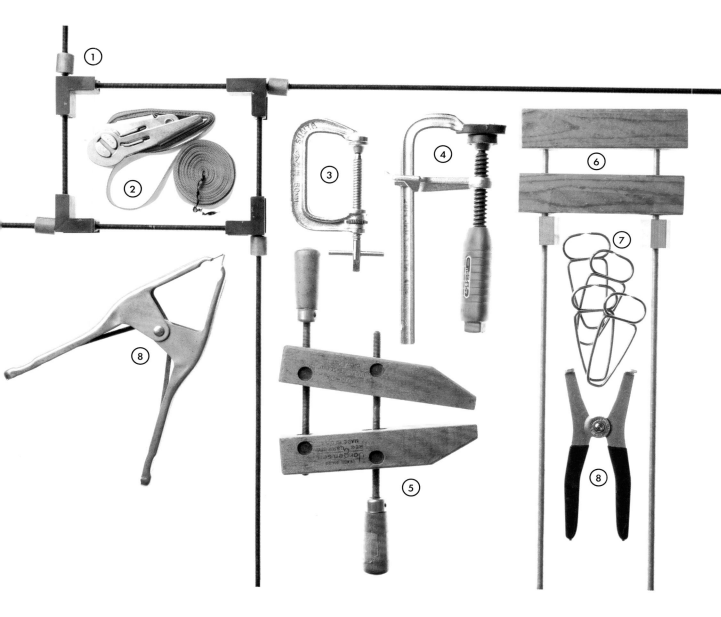

1 Four-way speed clamp: used for gluing joints on frames, etc.
2 Web clamp: useful for gluing joints on boxes, picture frames, etc. Ratchet type, can be firmly tightened.
3 C-shape clamp.
4 F-style clamp: convenient because of its large holding surface.

5 Handscrew clamp.
6 Custom gluing clamps.
7 and **8** Spring clamp kit.

Chapter 2
FRAMING

In this chapter, you will learn how to make frames using seven different types of woodworking joint. Frames form the basis of a variety of useful objects, from photo frames to cabinet doors. Some frames are more complex than others. For instance, with photo frames, in addition to the simple frame form, the back needs to be rabbeted to hold glass or acrylic and a backing board. A cabinet door frame also needs rabbets or notches to fit a panel (mitred inset panel), or glass. This chapter provides instructions for making photo frames using seven different types of woodworking joints, progressing in difficulty from Level 1 through to Level 7.

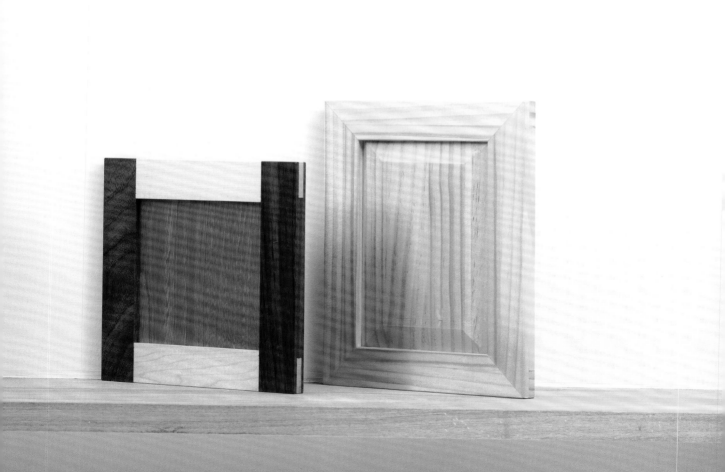

LEVEL 1
HALF LAP JOINT PHOTO FRAME

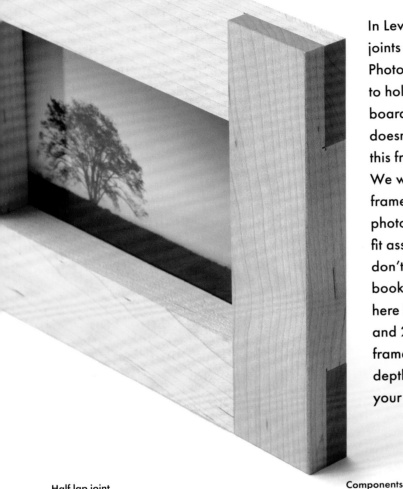

In Level 1, we will learn how to create half lap joints to make beautiful panoramic photo frames. Photo frames normally have rabbets on the back to hold acrylic/glass, a photo and a backing board. However, this particular photo frame doesn't have any rabbets at all. As you can see, this frame is very simple, but it still looks great. We will learn how to make rabbeted photo frames in the next level. Although simple, this photo frame clearly shows the highly accurate fit associated with the half lap joint. Accuracy, don't forget, is one of the main features of this book's unique methods. The photo frame made here is postcard-sized. The wood is 40mm wide and 20mm thick. The reason for such a thick frame is that we wanted to produce a sense of depth. That being said, please feel free to vary your chosen wood thickness.

Half lap joint

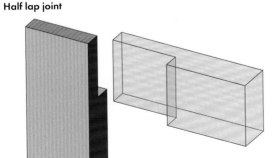

Components

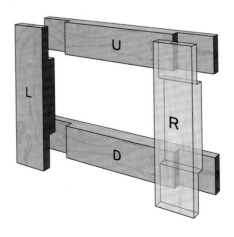

HALF LAP JOINT PHOTO FRAME PRODUCTION SEQUENCE

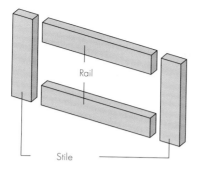

Rail

Stile

1 Cut out two pieces of wood, both stiles and rails, of the same dimension. Mark the top, bottom, left and right sides (see step 10 on page 45).

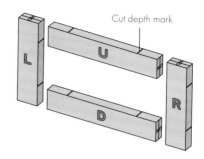

Cut depth mark

2 Mark cut depth. Add Xs and Os on the end grain (see steps 11 and 12 on page 45).

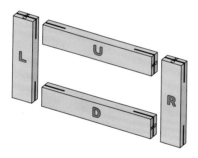

3 Use a ripping guide to cut vertically. Be sure to follow the rule: **'Insert a saw blade spacer if you see an O mark.'** (See step 21 on page 47, and step 8 on page 16.)

4 Use a cross-cut guide to cut off the unnecessary parts, marked with an X (see step 30 on page 48).

NOTE

When making frames, whether for a door or for photo frames, the two vertical boards are called 'stiles' and the two horizontal boards are called 'rails'. Stiles are visible all the way from top to bottom, while the rails appear to be sandwiched between the stiles. We call this type of structure 'stile dominant'. It is the industry standard when making frames.

HOW TO MAKE A HALF LAP JOINT

How to make a datum line

1 Mark a datum line on the straightest side of the wood. Remember that wood doesn't always have a constant width. Mark a datum line and try to cut at right angles from that line as much as possible. Here is a datum line on the material edge.

Cutting ends

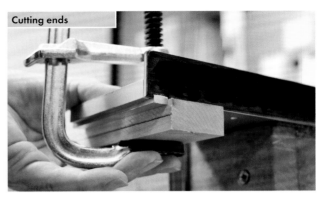

2 Cut off the material ends with the cross-cut guide. The photo shows the aluminium cross-cut guide being used to clamp up our piece, with the datum line facing forwards.

3 Here's the cut-off end piece.

Cutting the rails

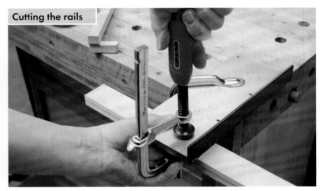

4 Face the cut-off end to the left, mark the required length and clamp while lining up the magnetic sheet. Remember that in this book's methods, when cutting wood, the desired length is that which is under the cross-cut guide.

5 Set the length hook (see page 25) to repeatedly cut your material to the exact same dimensions. Clamp the wood to the workbench with the hook against the end grain. To be sure of an exact fit, loosen the clamp, force the material up against the length hook, and re-clamp.

6 Butt the saw blade up against the magnetic sheet and saw off the material. Hold the saw softly and rip straight. Position your elbow as an extension of the saw blade, so that you will always rip straight.

7 After cutting, slide the remaining 'excess' wood over and place it against the length hook. Cut out the second piece (check for burrs first). To check for accuracy, lay the two pieces on top of each other and lightly touch both ends.

8 Of course, the cut edges will have burrs. Use a sanding block to remove them as these burrs could interfere with the length hook and prevent the material from being cut precisely.

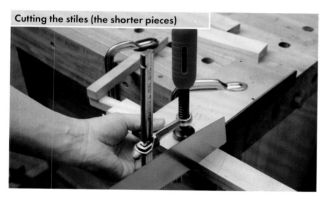

Cutting the stiles (the shorter pieces)

9 The same method as described above is used to cut out the stiles

10 Lay out all four pieces of wood. Write top, bottom, left, right, on each piece to show its position and to distinguish front from back. When clamping material to the ripping guide, it should be always clamped with the front side facing out.

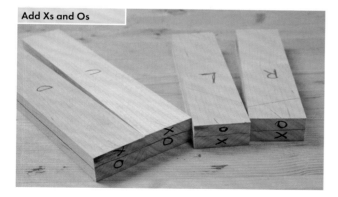

Add Xs and Os

11 We will make this frame according to the stile dominant ideal. Write Xs and Os on the end grains. Ignore the pencil lines between each X and O, since we just marked them for convenience (see step 2 on page 43).

12 Use the height of the corresponding piece (as in photo) to mark the edge of each piece (see step 2 on page 43).

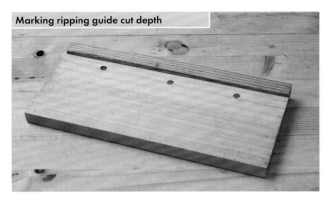

13 Here's the depth cut guide for setting the depth stop on our saw (see page 30).

14 Place the saw blade against the fence. Next, place the material on the blade, while maintaining contact between the teeth and fence, as shown.

15 Attach the depth stop to the saw blade with double-sided tape. This is the best way to control cut depth.

16 Fix the ripping guide to the workbench and attach the spacer with double-sided tape. Spacer thickness in this case is 10.3mm (9mm thick plywood + the magnetic sheet). That's about half the thickness of the material we are cutting.

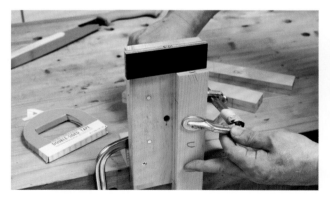

17 Clamp the rail piece to the ripping guide. The clamping position is a little below the pencil line you drew earlier. For both rail and stile pieces, always clamp with the front side of the material facing outwards. This is a very important rule!

18 Once the wood is clamped, you can draw the actual cutting line (in pen here). It's not necessary to draw this line, but we have done it for clarity.

19 The clamp has been removed to reveal the Xs and Os. The red line indicates where the saw will be cutting. You can see that it will be on the side marked with an X.

20 Clamp the material again. Note that I have substituted a digitally manipulated clear spacer for the real spacer here. The area marked with the O is hidden behind the spacer while the red line is in front of the spacer, on the area marked with an X.

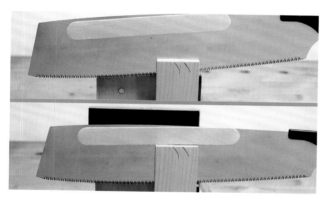

21 Rip vertically. Stop ripping when the depth stop hits the material and prevents further cutting. Don't force anything or the depth stop may fall off. Cut the opposite end of the wood in the same way (see step 3 on page 43).

22 Both ends of the two rails have been cut, as shown. The next step is to cut the stiles.

Cutting stiles

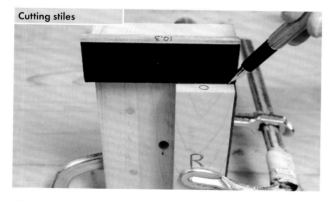

23 Clamp the stiles to the ripping guide front side out. This time, you can see an O in front of the spacer, unlike the rail piece. If you draw a line along the spacer, that will be the cutting line.

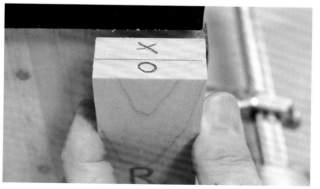

24 Here is the cutting line. When sawing, if the kerf is on the circle side, the thickness of the circle area will be reduced by the kerf width. That is why we need to make sure the kerf is on the X side.

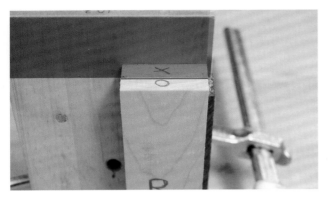

25 Here we can see the digitally manipulated spacer outline. If you cut in at this point, the saw blade will enter the O side of the cutting line (as shown in red) and the joint will not work.

26 To solve this problem, attach a saw blade spacer to the ripping guide. The spacer must be the same size as the saw blade you use for cutting. Dull blades work great as spacers.

27 Now we can see how the wood was clamped down. It has been shifted forwards by the thickness of the dull saw blade spacer.

28 Now the kerf will be on the X side when you make your cut. Remember, in our unique method, the rule is: **'If you can see the area marked with an O, insert a saw blade spacer'.**

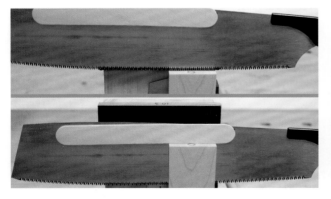

29 Cut until you reach the depth stop. Turn the pieces over and make cuts in the opposite ends of the stile pieces in the same manner.

Cut off the X-marked part (unnecessary part)

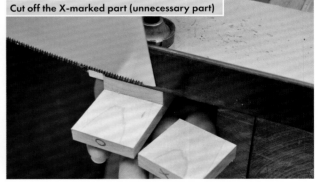

30 Now we will cut off the unnecessary parts with a cross-cut guide. To do this, we first need to decide where to cut. From page 49, step 31 onwards you will find a description of the method used to position the pieces to be cut (see also step 4 on page 43).

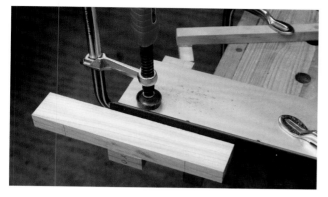

31 This is how to set the cut. All we have to do is set the actual stile piece over the X-marked section of the rail. Note that the length hook (to the rear) is set so we can precisely repeat the cut.

32 Place the stile on the rail and compare the side and end grains. Make sure there are no gaps or differences in the two pieces.

33 Cut into the rail to about half its thickness. Be careful not to overcut. Cut off all unnecessary X parts.

Dry fitting

34 Dry fit and check for gaps. Be sure to check to see if there is any leftover material on the inside corners, as this will need to be removed.

Planing inside edges

35 Before gluing, we need to plane what will be the inside surface of the photo frame, because otherwise it will be difficult to plane after gluing.

Fastening with glue

36 Use a silicone spatula to apply the glue. Once hardened, the glue can be cleanly peeled off the spatula so don't worry if it gets all gummed up.

37 When clamping, be sure to apply a square to each corner and check for right angles.

38 Plane both sides to a smooth finish.

39 Plane smooth the surrounding area. Here we are using a shooting board for stability (see page 162).

40 Bevel the entire outside edge of the frame.

41 If you want to display the photo frame in an upright position, don't forget to make a hole for the round bar to hold it upright.

42 Decide on the angle you want the picture frame to stand. Tilt the picture frame to the correct angle on the workbench, mark the round bar and cut.

43 Apply double-sided tape around the opening where we will attach an acrylic (or glass) plate.

44 Cut the acrylic plate, centre it and paste it around the top, bottom, left and right sides.

45 Cut off any overhanging double-sided tape with a box cutter.

46 Place your photo on the acrylic plate and secure all four corners with tape.

47 To make a wall hanging, temporarily place studs in three places. Wrap string around the two outer studs, and then push them in to hold the string tight. Pull out the centre stud and stick it in the wall to use as a hook for hanging the picture frame.

48 The project is complete. For the next level, we will make a rabbeted half lap joint frame that can hold the acrylic/glass, a photo and a backing board. This technique can be applied to cabinet doors with panels or glass inserts as well.

LEVEL 2
RABBETED HALF LAP JOINT PHOTO FRAME

For this level, we will use the Level 1 photo frame as a base, but we'll rabbet the back to create space for the acrylic, etc. Once mastered, this method can be applied not only to photo frames, but also to cabinet doors inlaid with acrylic, glass or wood panels. If the half lap joints are rabbeted all the way along the back side, the rail rabbets will be visible from the exterior of the frame, as shown in 'Incorrect rabbeted half lap joint' on page 53 (circled areas in figure 4). To avoid this, we overlap the rabbet by manipulating the half lap. In this level, the rails are processed first. When making half lap joints, spacer thickness for the ripping guide should be about half the material thickness. Here, the material is 19mm and the spacer is 10.3mm. Be sure to use a rabbeting guide (see page 186).

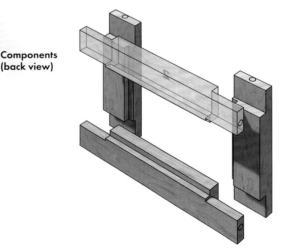

Components
(back view)

INCORRECT RABBETED HALF LAP JOINT

1 Photo frame (front side) with normal half lap joints.

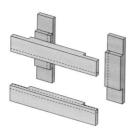

2 Once disassembled, the dotted lines are rabbeted.

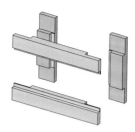

3 The yellow sections represent the rabbeted areas.

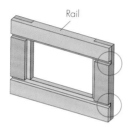

Rail

4 When reassembled, the rabbeted rails are visible from the outside (circled).

5 If you cut the half lap joint correctly, there will be no visible rabbet from the exterior (circled).

PRODUCTION SEQUENCE

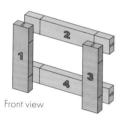

Front view

1 Cut the rails and stiles the same size. Place Xs and Os where necessary on end grain. Make a cut depth line (see step 2 on page 54).

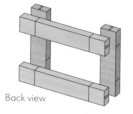

Back view

2 Materials are fixed with the front side facing the ripping guide (see step 3 on page 54).

3 Make cross-shaped cuts in the rails. Follow the rule: 'Whenever you see an O, insert a saw blade spacer'. (see step 10 on page 55).

4 Cut off parts you don't need with a cross-cut guide. Use calipers to measure the width (see step 13, page 56).

5 Mark lines on the stiles that match the measurements made with the calipers (see step 21 on page 57).

6 Cut vertically down to the white line (see step 23 on page 57).

7 Cut off unnecessary parts with the cross-cut guide (see step 24 on page 57).

8 Rabbet inside the perimeter with the rabbeting guide (step 31 on page 59).

HOW TO MAKE A RABBETED HALF LAP JOINT

1 Front side. The cut pieces temporarily laid out and numbered. This basic frame is 'stile dominant'. When clamping wood to the ripping guide, either clamp with every back side facing out or every front side facing out. Do not mix (see step 1 on page 53).

2 Back side. The wood has been reversed for marking. The lines indicating the ripping guide cut depth should be marked at this stage.

3 Back side. Add X and O marks and mark the approximate positions of the rail ends so that the correct part can be cut off and so the rabbet won't be visible from the exterior (see step 2 on page 53).

4 Attach the spacer (10.3mm) to the ripping guide with double-sided tape. **All the material that is to be clamped here should be clamped with the front side facing the guide and the back side facing out.**

5 When you clamp the rail piece, you should see the O in front of the spacer. Remember to follow the rule: **'If you can see the area marked with an O, insert a saw blade spacer'.**

6 Attach a thin stick to the depth stop. It is 40mm from the cutting edge because the material is 40mm wide. Rip vertically.

7 Here, I have cut to a depth of 40mm. The depth stop prevented me from cutting any further.

8 Clamp the wood on the edge vertically. Cut the side with the line at the approximate location where you want the rail piece end to be. Make sure the piece is facing the right direction!

9 Cut to a depth of 40mm.

10 This is what the cross-shaped cut should look like (see step 3 on page 53).

11 Cut the other end in the same way. In the picture, you can see that the line indicating the cut-off position is now reversed.

12 As before, make a cross-shaped cut to complete ripping on both ends of the two rail pieces.

13 Using the cross-cut guide, place the matching stile on the edge of the rail piece and align. Fixing the cut-off position by lining up the actual stile makes things much more accurate (see step 4 on page 53).

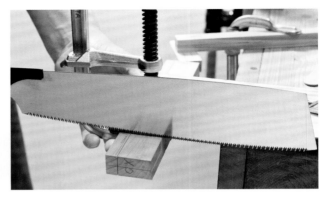

14 Set the length hook (seen in the background) and then cut off any unnecessary parts. Cut off all cross-shaped parts except the half lap section.

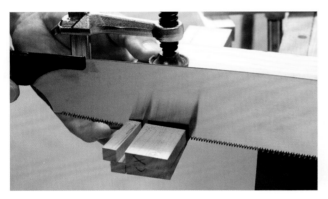

15 Both sections have been cut off.

16 Face the saw blade straight up and cut off the one remaining piece. This part (the notch) hides the rabbet from view when finished. Make sure the blade doesn't scratch the magnetic sheet when sawing in this position.

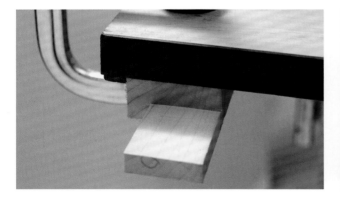

17 All unnecessary parts have now been cut off. You can see the notch now as well. This notch makes the rabbet, which will be done later, invisible from outside the frame.

18 Flip the piece and cut the other end. Thanks to the length hook, the cut position is automatically correct. For this end we need to cut off the opposite side for the notch, so point the saw straight down and cut.

19 The notch is complete.

20 Use calipers to pinch the rail edge, widthwise. Then, tighten the retaining screw on the calipers. There's no need to actually measure the width. This width becomes the depth of the stile rip (see step 4 on page 53).

21 Place the calipers directly on the stile and mark. This is the new cut depth. The line next to it would be the cut-out position if the stile piece wasn't notched (see step 5 on page 53).

22 Reattach the depth stop to the saw blade in its new position. This position is the same as the value on the calipers that you just used.

23 Rip vertically down to the stopper (see step 6 on page 53).

24 Cut off the X-marked area with the cross-cut guide. To position, just use the actual rail piece. Don't forget to set the length hook (see step 7 on page 53).

25 The unnecessary parts have now been cut off. If there is any leftover material in the corners there will be gaps in the joints, so make sure you clean everything up with a saw, chisel or box cutter.

26 Dry fit and check for gaps in the joints.

27 Before we assemble and complete the project, we must plane the inner perimeter.

28 Notches at both ends of the rail pieces that hide rabbeted gaps are made with 10.3mm thick spacers. If pieces are rabbeted along dotted lines, the rabbets won't be visible. This is called the 'rabbet range'.

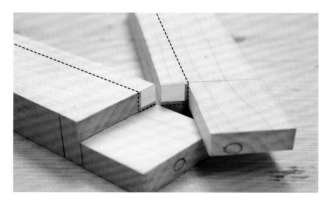

29 In this example, the rabbets are slightly smaller than the dotted lines, meaning we will cut out the yellow squares. For this reason, we need to use 7mm spacers (5.5mm thick MDF + a magnetic sheet).

Using rabbeting guide

30 Attach a 7mm thick spacer to the rabbeting guide. Position the spacer as shown in the photo.

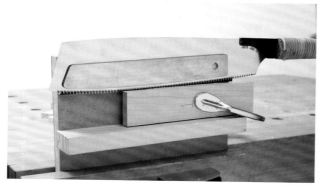

31 The wood is clamped and the saw blade has a brass plate (self-made) depth stop/weight. The cut depth will be about 7mm (see step 8 on page 53).

32 Lay the material on its side and cut out the rabbet. The cut-out is quite small, so you can either leave the magnetic sheet as it is or lower it a little and reattach.

33 Vertical and horizontal cuts meet, and the unwanted square part is removed.

Dry fitting

34 Rabbet all pieces this way.

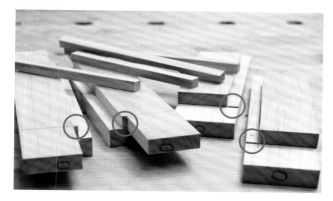

35 Here is the processed wood. The stile pieces are on the right and the rails are on the left. Both sets were processed a little smaller than the 'rabbet range' so you can see that they are just slightly stepped (circled).

36 Here is everything temporarily assembled again.

37 Stepped and uneven corners are caused by cutting a little smaller than the rabbet range. You can eliminate this by cutting with the maximum rabbet range. See the box opposite for an alternative, with grooves within the rabbet.

See the box opposite

GROOVES WITHIN THE RABBET

You can put grooves within the rabbet that can take panels of wood or glass. The one in the illustration can be used for a cabinet door.

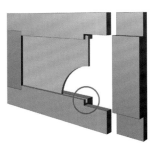

Planing

38 Use a planer to remove differences in thickness and to smooth out both the front and back.

39 Chamfer the perimeter. For details regarding attaching metal fittings to the photo frame, refer to step 43 on page 70.

refer to step 43 on page 70

40 The project is complete!

LEVEL 3
SPLINED MITRE JOINT PHOTO FRAME

When the wood is joined at a 45-degree angle, the end grain is hidden and has a clean and beautiful appearance. This is called a splined mitre joint. However, because the wood ends are glued together directly, they are relatively weak and will need reinforcement. To do this, after gluing, we make a cut from outside the corner and insert a thin plate (spline key) to reinforce the joint. This is called a keyed mitre joint or splined mitre joint. This is a difficult process because when you cut the wood at 45 degrees and put all four pieces together, there are always gaps in the joint. It is also difficult to cut both rail and stile for the spline key. To fix this, the book's unique methods use a guide with a mitre cut function (the aluminium cross-cut guide), a handmade length hook of at least 250mm, a self-made accurate guide and accessories.

Splined mitre joint

Components

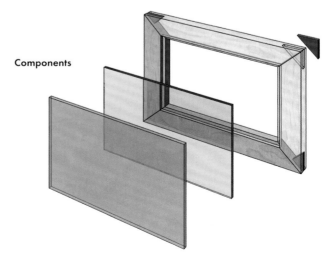

SPLINED MITRE JOINT PRODUCTION SEQUENCE

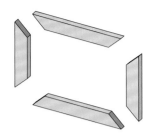

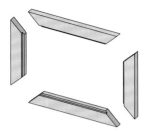

1 Cut each piece 4mm longer than it needs to be and mark 2mm in from the edge. Include a 45-degree line (see step 1 opposite).

2 Use the length hook to mitre 2mm in from the end (see step 6 opposite).

3 Use the rabbeting guide to rabbet the back of the photo frame (see step 10 on page 64).

4 Glue everything in place (see step 15 on page 65).

5 Use the Accurate Guide to cut grooves for spline keys (see step 22 on page 66).

6 Glue in the spline keys (see step 35 on page 69).

7 Plane (see step 38 on page 69).

8 Cut out the acrylic plate and backing board, and then attach the metal fittings (see steps 41 and 43 on page 70).

HOW TO MAKE A SPLINED MITRE JOINT

Cutting wood

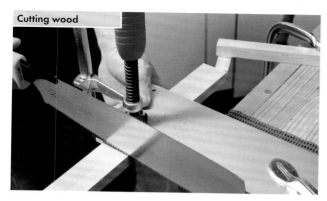

1 Use the aluminium cross-cut guide to cut and process 45-degree splined mitre joints. First, use the length hook to cut two rails and two stiles to the same dimensions. Cut 4mm longer than the finished length (see step 1 opposite).

2 After cutting out the pieces, use a pencil to mark the direction of 45-degree mitres. Each piece should be numbered and positioned accordingly.

45-degree mitre cuts

3 Make a mark 2mm in from the edge of the cut piece. This is where you will make the 45-degree cut.

4 Attach two 45-degree pins to the aluminium cross-cut guide. To install pins, just screw them in place away from the fence. See the aluminium cross-cut guide instruction manual for details.

5 Clamp the aluminium cross-cut guide to the workbench. Use a plate that is at least 4mm thick. The guide should be fixed at 45 degrees to the workbench, meaning directly out from the corner.

6 Align the edge of the material with the 2mm mark, along the magnetic sheet, so that material will be cut at 45 degrees. Fix with a clamp. Next, clamp the length hook while holding it against the material (see step 2 opposite).

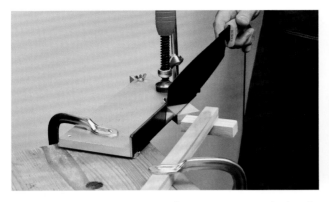

7 Before actually cutting, reset the piece up against the length hook to make sure it is correct.

8 With mitre cuts, clamping is delicate and can be easily ruined by awkward sawing. Remember to saw straight and use short strokes. To make mitres, maintain this set up and re-clamp everything while turning the pieces.

9 Fit rubber bands around the frame perimeter and make sure there are no gaps in the joints. If necessary, use a planer to modify.

10 Next, cut rabbets where acrylic board and backer board must fit. For the spacer here, I used a 5.2mm thick piece of 4mm plywood with a magnetic sheet attached (see step 3 on page 62).

11 Clamp a piece to the guide and attach a spacer about 2mm above it with double-sided tape. Attach the depth stop to the saw blade. This time set it about 6mm deep and make your vertical cut.

12 Fix the wood horizontally and cut off the unwanted part of the rabbet. The spacers are not repositioned here, but they can be moved closer to the wood for better accuracy if desired.

13 The unwanted part has been cut away and the cross section is clean. This is how all the pieces are rabbeted.

This photo frame with a staircase-like decoration was made with a rabbeting guide. It was created using two types of spacers of differing thickness.

Planing inside edges

14 It is best to finish the areas inside of the picture frame at this stage, as they will be difficult to finish after gluing. Here a Lie-Nielsen 60-1/2 block plane is used.

Gluing

15 Spring clamps are used to tighten the splined mitre joints. Use the special pliers to unwind them and release to stick the ends into the wood. These clamps create small holes, but they disappear when spline keys are inserted (see step 4 on page 62).

16 Clamp the tops and bottoms of the joints so there are no gaps.

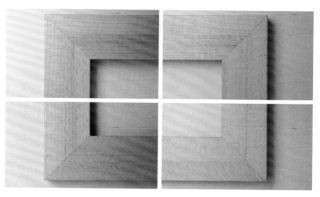

17 By using the aluminium cross-cut guide, we have gap-free mitre joints, as shown.

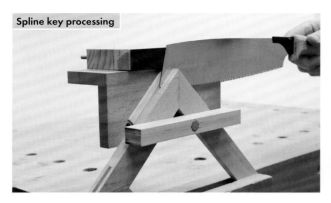

18 Spline keys act as reinforcement and decoration. Here I chose a dark-coloured teak (30 × 5mm) to contrast with the photo frame. Use the Accurate Guide to cut grooves of equal width to the thickness of the spline keys. See page 210 for instructions.

19 Use a speed square to draw lines that are slightly shallower than the key width.

20 Set the ruler and mark the material. This is the cut depth.

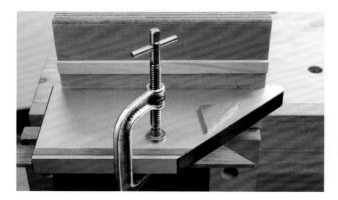

21 Cut out the teak spline keys. Here we are using an aluminium cross-cut/mitre cut jig, but any method can be used as long as you cut at 45 degrees.

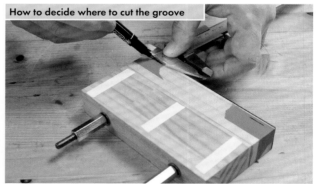

How to decide where to cut the groove

22 The frame material is 15mm thick, and a 5mm piece of teak makes up the key. Therefore, the first cut point is 5mm from the frame edge. To align the Accurate Guide, mark a black line 5mm from the magnetic sheet. Affix double-sided tape to the Accurate Guide's three fixing points (see step 5 on page 62).

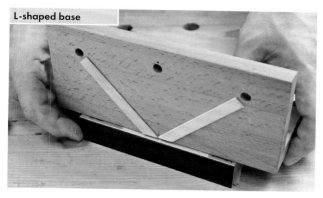

L-shaped base

23 Align the L-shaped base with the ink line of the Accurate Guide and fix with double-sided tape.

24 Attach the frame holding rod to the L-shaped base.

25 Pass the frame holding rod through the photo frame while it is fixed to a bench vice.

26 Secure the whole thing with wing nuts. Use your left hand to hold the photo frame between the holding rod and the L-shaped base and use your right hand to turn the wing nut. This will make things easier.

First cut

27 The Accurate Guide is sticking out 5mm from the L-shaped base, and that is the first cut point. Make sure that there is a spacer sandwiched in the Accurate Guide. With the spacer in place, the guide should be sticking out 5mm.

Pinch spline keys in guide

28 Cut down to the marked lines.

29 Remove the spacer, and now place two spline keys in the Accurate Guide. You are now ready to make the second cut.

Second cut

30 The second cut is made and the groove width is now set.

31 Now we need to remove the unnecessary part.

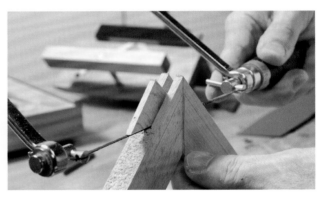

32 Use the coping saw to roughly cut out the unwanted part.

33 Finish the bottom with a chisel. If the bottom is even slightly raised, there will be a gap on the outside edge of the key. The trick here is to make the bottom slightly concave.

34 This completes the groove where the spline key will fit.

35 Apply adhesive inside the groove, insert the spline key and press down firmly so there is no gap (see step 6 on page 62).

36 I waited for the glue to harden while holding the keys down with clamps because one of the spline keys was floating a little.

37 Trim off any overhanging areas.

38 Finish off the outer perimeter by planing the edges of the spline keys (see step 7 on page 62).

39 If it's difficult to finish at right angles by hand (as shown in the previous step), you can use the planer on a shooting board as shown.

40 Finish the front and back surfaces with a plane.

41 Cut out 1mm acrylic sheeting based on the frame size (see step 8 on page 62).

42 We also cut a 4mm plywood backer.

43 Attach the frame hardware (see photo on page 52).

44 To complete the project, apply sanding sealer, then sand with sandpaper or steel wool before spraying with a matte clear lacquer.

LEVEL 4
MITRED HALF LAP JOINT PHOTO FRAME

This is a splined mitre joint when viewed from the front and a half lap joint when viewed from the back. The large bonding area makes it really strong. It isn't necessary to reinforce with spline keys like the splined mitre joint (see page 61). For the ripping guide, use spacers close to half the wood thickness. Use a self-made mitre-cutting guide for the 45-degree angle mitre cut. For details on how to make it, refer to 'Mitre cutting guide' on page 172 (this guide is actually useful for a variety of situations).

Stile

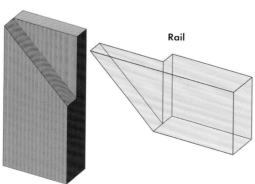

Rail

Components

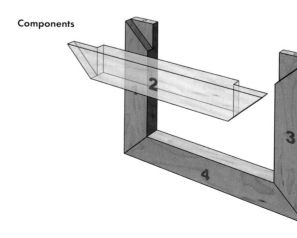

MITRED HALF LAP JOINT PRODUCTION SEQUENCE

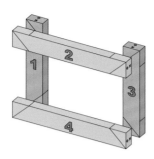

1 Cut the wood, mark the cut direction lines and add Xs and Os to the end grain (see step 1 opposite).

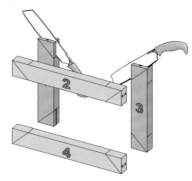

2 Cut into the stile piece at a 45-degree angle (see step 2 opposite).

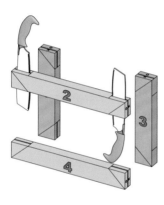

3 Make a cut in the rail piece. Follow the rule: **'When you see an O, insert the saw blade spacer'.** (see step 6 opposite).

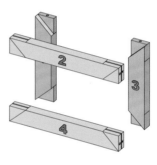

4 Use the mitre cutting guide to cut off the stile piece at 45 degrees (see step 8 on page 74).

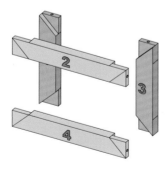

5 Use the cross-cut guide to cut off the unwanted part of the rail piece (see step 14 on page 75).

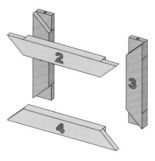

6 Mitre cut the rail piece with the mitre cutting guide (see step 16 on page 75).

HOW TO MAKE A MITRED HALF LAP JOINT

1 Start with cutting out the parts. Mark with Xs and Os and add cut depth marks, etc. (see step 1 opposite). The truncated areas at both rail ends seen above are marked with Xs. These are the bases for inserting the other Xs and Os.

2 Start by cutting the stiles. Remove the fence from the ripping guide to secure the wood at an angle. Use a spacer that is close to half the material thickness. In this case, the material is 19mm and the spacer is 10.3mm (see step 2 opposite).

3 Clamp the stile piece at an angle in the ripping guide. The saw blade spacer is not used because the X mark is visible in front of the spacer.

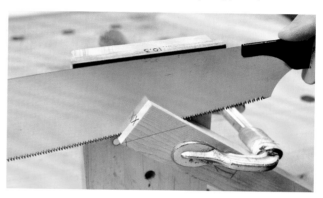

4 Use the saw to cut from the corner to the marked line, cutting down to the 45-degree line.

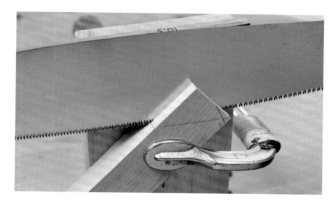

5 When cutting the other side, the tilt direction is reversed. As before, cut from the wood corner to the marked line. Cut all the stile pieces in the same way.

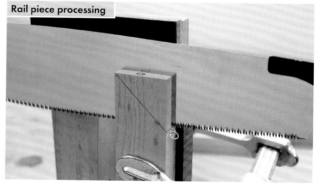

Rail piece processing

6 Instead of cutting in at a 45-degree angle, cut like a normal half lap joint. However, you must also replace the removed fence. Apply the motto: **'If you can see the area marked with an O, insert a saw blade spacer'** (see step 3 opposite).

Using the mitre cutting guide

7 Stile and rail cuts can be seen by inserting pieces of paper. In the photo, piece no.1 is the stile and piece no.2 is the rail.

8 Cut off the unnecessary part by clamping at 45 degrees. Do not cut through the entire piece, cut the half that has already been ripped with the ripping guide (see step 4 on page 72).

9 Place the T-shaped stopper on the corner of wood. Align the wood face with the long face of the T-shaped stopper.

10 Place the mitre cutting guide. Slide the guide fence along until the magnetic sheet surface touches the T-shaped stopper. This means that you have set the exact cutting position.

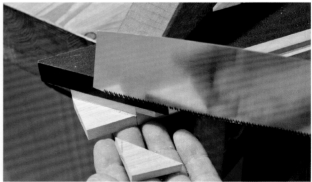

11 Clamp the mitre cutting guide and the wood together. You can use wood screw clamps here just like tweezers, although you could also use F-style clamps.

12 Cut the mitre.

13 If there is any leftover material inside the cut corners, there will be gaps in the joints, so be sure to clean the corners with a box cutter or chisel.

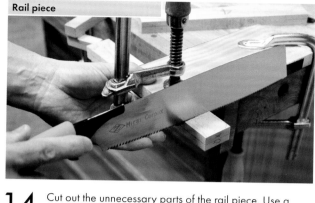

Rail piece

14 Cut out the unnecessary parts of the rail piece. Use a cross-cut guide to cut at a right angle instead of mitre cutting. Determine the cut position with the actual piece of wood and set the length hook as well (see step 5 on page 72).

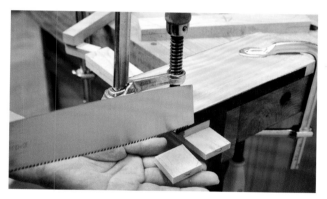

15 Cut off the unnecessary part. If there is any leftover material in the corner, remove it. After this, the part will be mitred.

16 Turn the rabbeted part so that it faces downwards. We will place the mitre cutting guide on top and mitre cut (see step 6 on page 72).

17 Place the T-shaped stopper on the material corner.

18 Place the mitre cutting guide on top and slide until the magnetic sheet surface touches the T-shaped stopper. Then, fix in that position.

19 Clamp securely.

20 Cut the mitre.

21 The other end is cut in the same way, using the mitre cutting guide in reverse. The photo shows the clamped wood and the mitre cutting guide from below.

22 Make a mitre cut. Cut all the rail pieces in this way.

23 This is the completed joint, shown.

24 Temporarily assemble the frame with rubber bands to check for gaps in the joints. If any gaps are found, correct them.

25 Use a shoulder plane to scrape off the mitred surface and correct any gaps.

26 With a planer, smooth the area around the inside perimeter. It's best to do this now, as it's difficult to do after gluing.

27 Glue the pieces together. Use belt clamps to tighten the periphery. Then, use C-clamps and clamping plates to prevent offsets from forming at the corners. The entire piece is then sanded and finished.

LEVEL 5
MITRED HALF LAP JOINT WITH GROOVE OR RABBETED FRAME

In this section using the back of the Level 4 frame, we will learn how to rabbet, for the glass insertion, and we will also learn to groove, for panel insertion with a mitred inset panel. Both grooving and rabbeting are done in the same way. Here, using a groove planer, we will process the grooves and insert the panels.

Mitred half lap joint

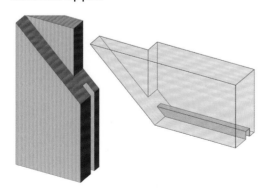

Components (back view)

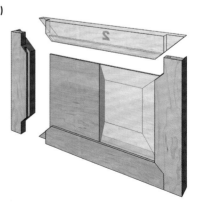

MITRED HALF LAP JOINT PRODUCTION SEQUENCE

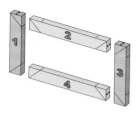

1 Cut out the pieces and mark an O or an X on the end grain. Look at the non-mitred part to decide which (see step 4 on page 80).

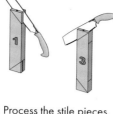

2 Process the stile pieces, making 45-degree angle cuts with a ripping guide (see step 5 on page 80).

3 Fix the material lengthwise in the ripping guide and cut down to the 45-degree line (see step 10 on page 81).

4 Cut off unwanted parts with the mitre cutting guide. Three unwanted parts will be cut off in a single area (see step 12 on page 81).

5 Copy the width of the area that is left onto calipers. This will be the cut depth into the rail (see step 18 on page 82).

6 Work on the rail pieces. Copy caliper dimensions directly onto the wood (see step 19 on page 83).

7 Make cross-shaped cuts, ripping vertically. It's useful to attach a depth stop here (see step 20 on page 83).

8 Use the cross-cut guide to cut off the back half at right angles. Use a length hook (see step 26 on page 84).

9 Cut off the front half with the mitre cutting guide (see step 29 on page 84).

10 Dry fit and check the entire structure. Clean up corners and correct any gaps in the fit with a planer (see step 33 on page 85).

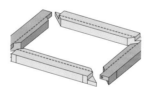

11 View from the back. Rabbeting and grooves can be machined within the dotted lines (see step 34 on page 85).

12 If you use the rabbeting guide (see page 186) to rabbet, you can just drop the glass plate in (see step 36 on page 85).

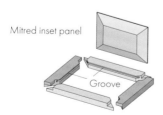

Mitred inset panel

Groove

13 If grooved, the mitred inset panel can be inserted and this will become a door (see step 37 on page 86).

14 Here it is with the mitred inset panel inserted (see step 40 on page 86).

HOW TO MAKE A MITRED HALF LAP JOINT

1 The photo shows a mitred half lap joint from 'Framing', Level 4. The mirror behind shows the back side. As you can see, it has a half lap joint.

2 This time, a panel is inserted into the frame. The mirror shows a stepped back side where the panel grooves aren't visible from the outside.

3 For the 45-degree mitre cut, we will be using our custom-made mitre cutting guide. Please refer to the mitre cutting guide on page 172 for instructions.

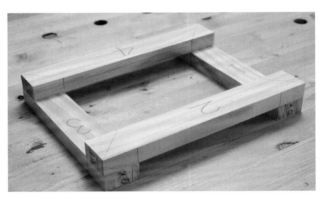

4 The material used here is 18mm thick. Cut out the stiles and rails and mark them. Place Xs and Os on the end grain (see step 1 on page 79).

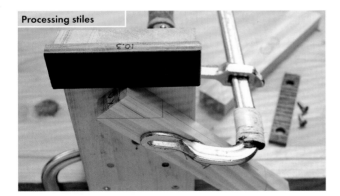

Processing stiles

5 Use a spacer that is approximately half the wood thickness. We used 10.3mm here. Remove the fence from the ripping guide and clamp the wood at an angle (see step 2 on page 79).

6 Make a 45-degree angle cut from the wood corner to the marked line.

7 To cut the other end, tilt the piece in the opposite direction and clamp. This is how you make cuts in all stiles.

8 After making a 45-degree angle cut, clamp the material vertically.

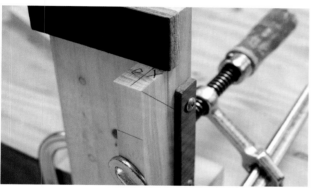

9 Clamp the inside of the frame against the ripping guide.

10 Cut down to a 45-degree line (see step 3 on page 79).

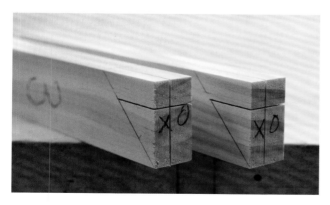

11 Cut all the stile pieces in a cross-shape.

Using the mitre cutting guide

12 Set the mitre cutting guide. The acrylic T-shaped stopper is used here as well, though not shown in the photo. Make sure the X mark is on top. Cut off all the pieces except those marked with Os (see step 4 on page 79).

13 Cut off the top two unnecessary parts.

14 The third piece is cut with the blade in an upright position. The contact area between the saw and the magnetic sheet will become smaller, so rip straight while holding it with your finger.

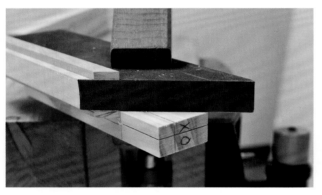

15 Flip the wood and set the mitre cutting guide in the opposite orientation.

16 Cut off all three unwanted portions. Again, the third cut should be vertical.

17 These are the completed stiles after the removal of unnecessary parts. If there are any leftovers in the corners, clean them up with a box cutter or chisel.

18 Pinch the edge of the completed stile piece with calipers and set the retaining screw. There is no need to measure, just set the width on the calipers (see step 5 on page 79).

19 Copy the caliper value directly onto the rail piece. This position will be the cut depth when ripping vertically (see step 6 on page 79).

20 Use the ripping guide to cut vertically. The O mark can be seen in front of the spacer, so you know you will sandwich a saw blade spacer. We will also return the ripping guide fence to its original position (see step 7 on page 79).

Using a depth stop

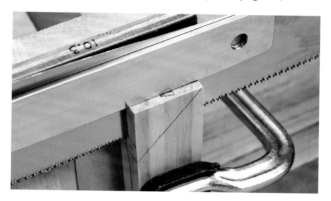

21 Copy the caliper value onto the saw blade as well and attach the depth stop with double-sided tape. The photo shows one I made myself from a brass plate.

22 Cut until the depth stop touches end grain. Unlike stiles, rails aren't clamped diagonally and cut at a 45-degree angle.

23 Clamp the wood vertically.

24 Cut down to the 45-degree line.

25 Make cross cuts through all the rails.

26 Use the cross-cut guide to cut off the X-marked side. Determine the cutting position by matching the actual piece with the stile. Use a length hook (see step 8 on page 79).

27 Cut off the unnecessary parts. Here I have done two of the cut-offs, as shown.

28 Here, the rails have been cut to the centreline.

29 Now make mitre cuts. Use the mitre cutting guide and T-shaped stopper to position the material (see step 9 on page 79).

30 After clamping the O-marked section, facing up, cut into it at 45 degrees and cut off the unnecessary parts. I used a straight-toothed replacement blade saw with a fine blade.

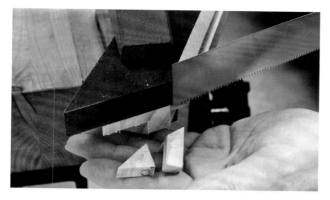

31 Here are the cut-offs, as shown.

32 Cut off the other side in the same way.

Assembly

33 Check the joints for gaps. If necessary, correct them with a planer, chisel or a similar tool (see step 10 on page 79).

34 This is the back side of the frame. Grooves aren't visible from the outside if notched or grooved within the dotted line as in step 11 on page 79.

35 Plane the surface of the frame's inner perimeter.

36 Cut a rabbet or groove in the yellow area from the photo. From here on, we will be grooving (see step 12 on page 79).

37 Use a groove planer with a 4mm-wide blade. Fix the wood to the workbench edge with double-sided tape, supported from behind with backup material. Set the groove cut depth stop to 5mm (see step 13 on page 79).

38 All pieces have been grooved.

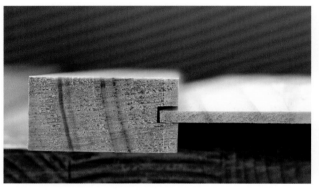

39 Fit the raised panel into the groove.

40 Glue the raised panel in place. No glue is applied to the raised panel itself. After gluing, sand and finish the entire raised panel (see step 14 on page 79).

RAISED PANEL FABRICATION

This section describes how to cut mitred panels. I used a 9mm thick board and a 60½ block plane. Just fix the fence at 30mm from the edge of the board and scrape. Shave until one side of the bottom of the planer touches the workbench and the other side touches the fence. This will result in the shape shown in the photo. When cutting, shave in the following order: wood edge, wood end, wood edge, wood end. Try different thicknesses of boards and different types of planers as needed.

LEVEL 6
BRIDLE JOINT FRAME

This joint looks difficult, but it is surprisingly easy to create using the techniques in this book. Since the two materials fit tightly together, you rarely have to make adjustments with a planer or chisel. That being said, making this joint is a time-consuming process using conventional hand tools. You will need a coping saw and chisel, in addition to the usual ripping guide and cross-cut guide. For the saw, use a Japanese flush-cut straight-toothed saw. This joint separates the wood into three sections. Note that the parts don't have to be equal. Adjust the spacer thickness so that the width of the concave part (slot) of the stile is wider than the width of your chisel.

Bridle joint

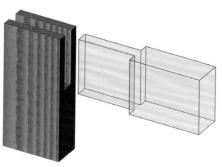

Components

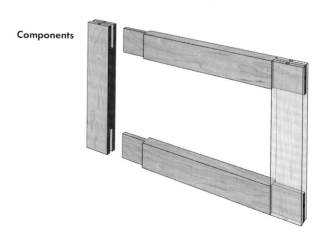

BRIDLE JOINT PRODUCTION SEQUENCE

1 Cut out the wood and mark it, putting Xs and Os on the end grain (see step 1 opposite).

2 Make incisions on the stiles. Turn the pieces over and make similar cuts. This will make two sets of parallel cuts (see step 4 opposite).

3 Make incisions in the rails as well. At this point, the nearest mark to the ripping guide spacer is an O, so insert a saw blade spacer (see step 7 on page 90).

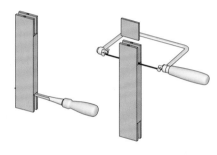

4 Roughly cut off the unnecessary stile parts with a coping saw and finish with a chisel (see step 10 on page 90).

5 Cut off the unnecessary rail parts with a cross-cut guide (see step 12 on page 90).

6 The project is complete.

HOW TO MAKE A BRIDLE JOINT

1 Cut two pieces to the same length using a cross-cut guide and a length hook. Mark with Xs and Os and cut depth positions. Walnut is used here for stiles and maple for rails. Note that the two materials must be the same thickness (see step 1 opposite).

2 Attach the depth stop and match the wood width with the actual piece.

Stile processing

3 Fix the stile piece to the ripping guide. The 15mm-thick wood divided into three equal parts is 5mm. We used 4.4mm-thick spacers. You can see an X and an O mark in front of the spacer, but the closest is the X mark, so the saw blade spacer won't be needed.

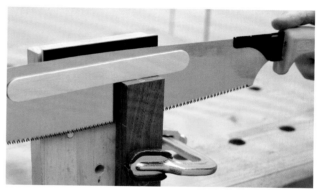

4 Cut until the depth stop touches the material (see step 2 opposite).

5 Turn the piece over and clamp it with the other side facing the guide.

6 Cut. (At this point, the saw blade got caught in the wood, so I am ripping with both hands.)

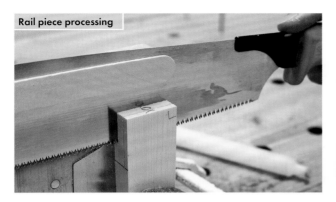

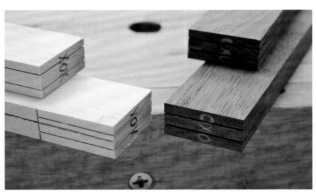

7 When the rail is fixed to the ripping guide, the mark nearest the spacer is the O, meaning that the saw blade spacer is placed between them. At this point I applied candle wax to both sides of the blade to stop it getting caught (see step 3 on page 88).

8 Both the stiles and the rails are now cut. Now, remove the X-marked stile material with a coping saw and chisel. Cut off the X-marked rail material with the cross-cut guide.

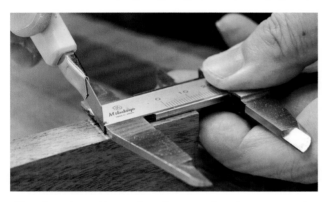

9 Copy the width onto the calipers, marking the position with a box cutter. This is done only on the two stile pieces, and this line is called 'the baseline'.

10 Use a coping saw to roughly cut out the X-marked section. Cut a few mm above the baseline (see step 4 on page 88).

11 Use a chisel to cut a little at a time. Gradually bring the cut closer to the baseline. In the beginning, cut both sides so the inside is slightly raised. As you progress, gradually cut horizontally and finally cut slightly downwards so that there will be no gaps when the joint is finished.

12 With the cross-cut guide, cut off the X-marked sections on both the rail pieces. Use the stile piece to find the rail baseline and apply the length hook at the opposite end (see step 5 on page 88).

13 Flip the piece and cut off the X-marked section on the other side. The photo shows the bottom cut-off part, and the X-marked section being cut off. This completes the process.

14 This frame fits perfectly and doesn't require any adjustment. This is one of the key features of the unique methods in this book.

15 After gluing, plane the frame.

16 The bridle joint is finished.

LEVEL 7
GROOVED BRIDLE JOINT FRAME (MITRED INSET PANEL)

In this section, we will use a groove planer to make sure that the grooves (where the panels fit into the Level 6 bridle joints) are not visible from the outside. As usual, the stiles and rails are marked, Xs and Os are added and work begins with the rails. The wood is 15mm thick, so we will use 4.4mm spacers, as that is close enough to the value needed to produce three equal parts.

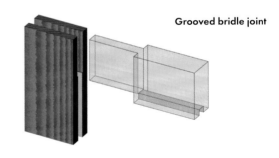

Grooved bridle joint

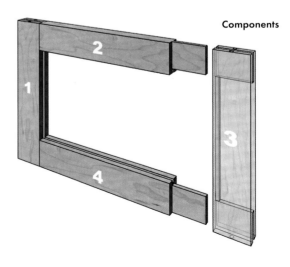

Components

GROOVED BRIDLE JOINT (MITRED PANEL) PRODUCTION SEQUENCE

1 Cut out the wood and mark it. Mark Xs and Os on the end grain.

2 Make three vertical cuts (see step 1 on page 94).

3 Cut off the unnecessary parts and measure the tenon width with calipers. This is how deep the stile piece will be cut (see step 5 on page 94).

4 Make two cuts in the stile down to the depth of the caliper measurement (see step 10 on page 95).

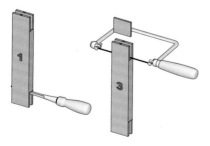

5 Remove the unwanted parts roughly with a coping saw and finish with a chisel (see step 12 on page 95).

Grooves

6 Cut grooves in the stiles and rails (see step 14 on page 96).

HOW TO MAKE A GROOVED BRIDLE JOINT (MITRED PANEL)

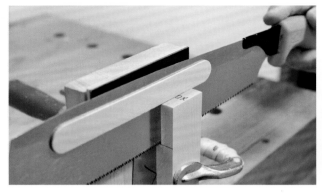

1 Attach a depth stop at the width of the joining piece and cut rail pieces. The spacer is marked with an O just in front of the spacer, so the rule of: **'If you can see the area marked with an O, insert a saw blade spacer'** applies (see step 2 on page 93).

2 After the first cut is made, turn the material over and re-clamp it.

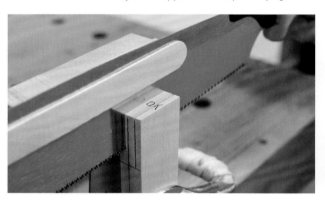

3 Make the second incision.

4 Clamp the wood vertically and make a third cut. The incision is on the inside. I cut with a saw blade spacer, but it doesn't affect the fit. Either way is fine.

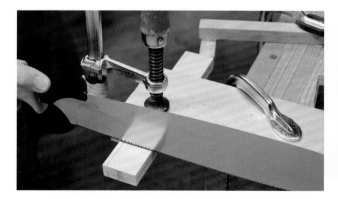

5 Use the cross-cut guide to remove the unnecessary parts. Use a length hook (see step 3 on page 93).

6 Turn the wood over and cut off all unwanted parts. Use the saw blade in the vertical or horizontal position, whichever is necessary.

7 Before and after cutting off the unnecessary parts.

8 Copy the hole width onto the calipers. This width is the depth to be cut into the stile piece next.

9 Use a depth stop here as well. Use an oil-based pen to copy the caliper measurement onto the saw blade and attach the stopper.

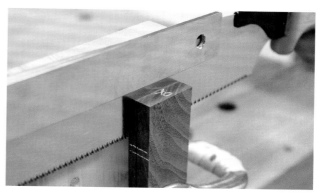

10 Make a cut in the stile. The mark in front of the spacer is an X, so a saw blade spacer isn't needed (see step 4, page 93).

11 Flip the piece of wood over and cut again.

12 After roughly cutting off the unnecessary parts with a coping saw, scribe the baseline with a chisel and finish cutting (see step 5, page 93).

13 The slots are now complete.

14 These are the completed mortices and tenons. Cut grooves in the green square areas (see step 6 on page 93).

Grooving

15 Attach backup material to the workbench to support the stiles and rails from behind.

16 Attach the stile to the workbench. The stile and front of the workbench should be flush (flat). Groove with a groove cutter.

17 Once the grooving is finished, plane the inside surface of the frame. It's best to do this now because it will be too difficult to finish after gluing.

18 Groove the rail. You can see a little craft stick stopper attached to the workbench in front of the material to prevent it from moving.

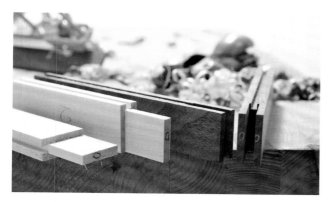

19 Grooves have been cut into all the pieces.

20 Assemble the frame and dry fit the panel.

21 Glue the joints. The panel is not glued. After this, plane and finish the panel face.

22 By changing the thickness of the spacers using this book's unique methods, larger joints can be processed in the same manner as described above.

Chapter 3
MAKING BOXES

Making boxes forms the basis of woodworking; boxes are not only for storage, but can also be used as cabinet casings. If you use the techniques in this chapter to make a cabinet casing, and the framing techniques learned in Chapter 2 to make the doors, you will be able to make a truly great piece of furniture. Make sure to have fun as you improve your woodworking skills by making the wooden boxes presented here.

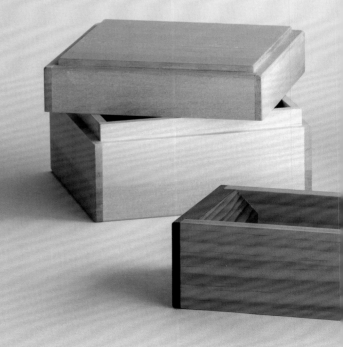

LEVEL 1
RABBET JOINT BOX

A rabbet joint box is formed by simply rabbeting both ends of the two end boards. Floor plate grooves aren't used here. Instead, we will introduce a separate simple method for the floor plate. First though, we'll look at all the production sequence diagrams and some photos before moving on to creating the box.

Structural drawing

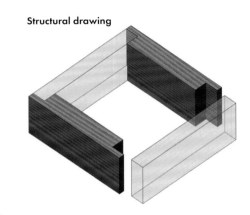

PRODUCTION SEQUENCE DIAGRAM FOR RABBET JOINT BOX

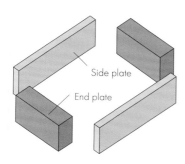

Side plate

End plate

1 Cut out the end and side plates. Mark Xs and Os in the correct positions on the end grain of the end plates. The same thickness of wood can be used for the sides and ends (see steps 1 and 4 on page 102).

2 Fix the outside of the end plate to the guide, facing inwards, and then rip vertically. Attach a depth stop to the saw blade (see step 2 on page 102).

3 Use the cross-cut guide to cut off the unnecessary parts. Also, be sure to use a length hook (see step 5 on page 102).

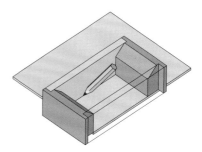

4 Cut the top portion of the end plates at an angle. This process isn't necessary, but it makes for a lovely accent (see step 9 on page 103).

5 Glue the plates together. Press each of the plates down firmly against the workbench so that the bottom of the box is flat (see step 11 on page 103).

6 Align one corner of the floor plate material with a box corner and trace out the floor plate outline (see step 13 on page 104).

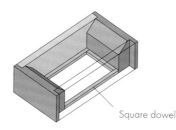

Square dowel

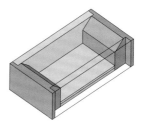

7 Cut out the floor plate by following the L-shaped line from step 6 (see also step 13 on page 104).

8 Glue thin square dowels around the bottom edge of the box (see step 14 on page 104).

9 Drop in the floor plate and glue (see step 18 on page 104).

HOW TO MAKE A RABBET JOINT BOX

1 Cut the wood and arrange it in a box shape. Write numbers 1–4, and Xs/Os, in the correct positions on the top, bottom, left and right sides. Different thicknesses of wood were used here but they can be the same if you wish (see step 1 on page 101).

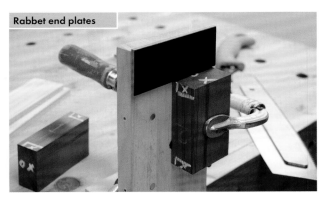

Rabbet end plates

2 Clamp the end plate into the rabbeting guide with the outside facing the guide. Use spacers no thicker than one third of the end plate. This will increase the side plate bonding area and make the box stronger (see step 2 on page 101).

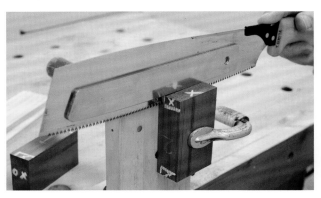

3 If you use a depth stop, there is no need to mark a depth line. The cut depth must be the side plate thickness.

4 All end plates have been cut (see step 1 on page 101).

5 Use the cross-cut guide to remove unnecessary parts. Use the side plate as a guide to determine where to cut (see step 3 on page 101).

6 Use a length hook when cutting off unnecessary parts. In this case the end plates are too short and hidden under the cross-cut guide so we can attach a block of scrap wood as a temporary stopper – note that the scrap block should be thicker than the end plate.

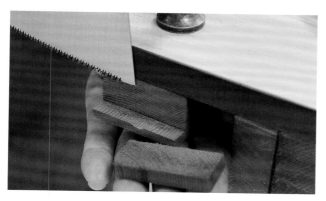

7 Cut off the unwanted part on one end, flip the material and place it against the end block. That way you can cut both ends to the same dimension.

8 The rabbeting process is complete. At this point it is best to check for leftover material in the corner. If you find any, be sure to remove it with a box cutter or a chisel.

9 Use a planer to diagonally carve the inside edge of each end plate. As mentioned before, this isn't necessary (see step 4 on page 101).

10 Dry fit, apply rubber bands and make sure there are no inside corner gaps. This is the last chance to inspect your work. Note, the bottom needs to be flat when gluing. Fortunately, any misalignment along the top can be corrected with a planer.

11 Apply adhesive to the end plate rabbets. After clamping, check that everything inside is perpendicular and, if necessary, apply force on the diagonal to correct any problems (see step 5 on page 101).

12 After the glue has set, lightly plane the bottom of the box to remove any bumps or extra glue.

13 Align a corner of plywood with the inside corner of the box. Draw pencil lines in an L-shape. Mark the side and end plate positions so that the floor plate will not be reversed when inserted. Cut out the floor plate (see steps 6 and 7 on page 101).

Gluing dowels

14 Make a base for the floor plate with thin square dowels. Glue them on all four inner sides. Align the bottom of the square dowel with the bottom of the box, apply instant glue and press evenly with your fingers (see step 8 on page 101).

Floor plate

15 If the floor plate is too large, use a planer to correct it. The floor plate is marked so that it is always inserted in the right direction. Make sure you know which side of the floor plate to shave down by marking it.

16 Test the floor plate again and again, checking and correcting as you go.

17 This is the bottom of the box. You can see that the narrow square dowel is supporting the floor plate.

18 Glue down the floor plate to complete the box (see step 9 on page 101).

LEVEL 2
CASE MITRE JOINT BOX

The *Inro* is a particular type of box with a special lid. The lid and body fit together tightly, without hinges, using what is called the *Hon-Inro* mechanism. The *Hon-Inro* mechanism involves mating the lid and box together with rabbeted risers and shoulders. Another mechanism, *Tsuke-Inro*, uses separate plates to make risers and glues them inside the box. For this project, we first need to cut the lid and box from a single board. Then we can connect the lid and box plates with masking tape and mitre both ends with the case mitre cutting guide. Also, use the case mitre cutting guide for the 45-degree cuts. See page 172 for case mitre cutting guide construction.

Structural drawing

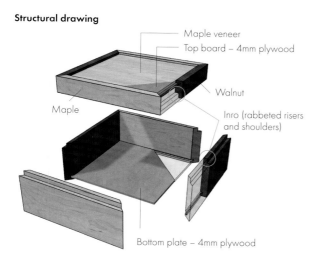

Maple veneer
Top board – 4mm plywood
Walnut
Maple
Inro (rabbeted risers and shoulders)
Bottom plate – 4mm plywood

PRODUCTION SEQUENCE FOR CASE MITRE JOINT BOX

Lid

Box

1 Cut out the wood for the lid and box in advance (see step 1 opposite).

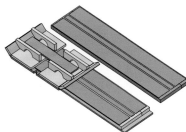

2 Make the lid and box into a single piece using masking tape. Set the guide plate and cut with the case mitre cutting guide (see step 2 opposite).

3 After cutting all four pieces at the correct angles, remove the masking tape and separate the lid from the body.

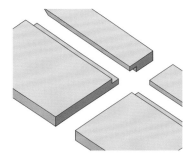

4 Cut the rabbets (steps) on both the lid and shoulders, as shown. The blue area shows the cross-section, and the steps are cut in the directions shown (see step 9 on page 108).

5 Make grooves for the lid top plate and body bottom plate (see step 28 on page 111).

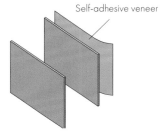

Self-adhesive veneer

6 Cut out the top and bottom board. Attach a sheet of self-adhesive veneer to the top board and plane off a thin layer around the edge on the back side (see step 32 on page 112).

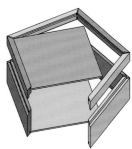

7 Glue everything up (see step 35 on page 112).

HOW TO MAKE A CASE MITRE JOINT BOX

1 Start by cutting pieces for the lid and body. Cut both the brown walnut and white maple into two pieces, as shown. The pieces are equal length because we are making a square box (see step 1 opposite).

2 Mask the lid and body pieces together. Mask all the way across, not just at the joints. If you don't, there will be small differences in height that can greatly affect the case mitre cutting guide's accuracy once it's clamped in place (see step 2 opposite).

3 Mark 45-degree lines on the right and left sides. The distance between the two lines is the length of the box side panels. You can see that the wood is placed on top of some fibre board to stop the saw from cutting into the work table.

4 Align the case mitre cutting guide with the lines and clamp.

5 Now, clamp the case mitre cutting guide on the other end and attach bridging material. Use double-sided tape to fasten both the left and right case mitre cutting guide pieces. We are making a square box, so we'll cut all four pieces using this configuration.

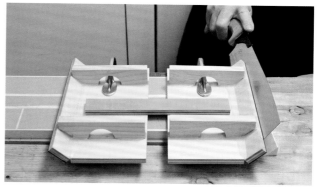

6 Make a 45-degree cut on one side. The saw blade is tilted at 45 degrees, so lean your body as well.

7 Cut the other side. This is how all the side panels are cut.

8 Dry fit with rubber bands to make sure there are no gaps.

Processing rabbeted risers and shoulders

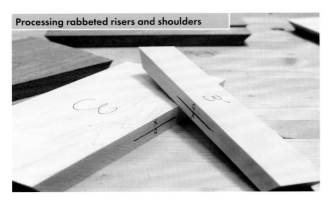

9 Process the rabbeted risers and shoulders for the lid and body. This is a 'lengthwise rabbeting' process. The lid exterior is marked with Os, and the inside of the body is also marked with Os (see page 43 and also step 4 on page 106).

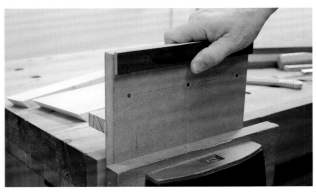

10 We'll use the rabbeting guide here. The wood is 15mm thick, so I used 7mm spacers – almost half the wood thickness.

11 For this part, we will be fixing both the lid and body of the box to the jig with the outer side facing outwards. Place the body in the jig first. Note that the saw blade spacer isn't inserted as the X is visible in front of the spacer.

12 Attach the depth stop, set to 10mm, and cut until you hit the stopper.

13 Cut the walnut in the same way.

14 When the depth stop hits the material, the saw blade will slip and stop cutting. This allows us to easily cut to the specified depth.

15 Here's the view from another angle. You can clearly see the 10mm deep cut.

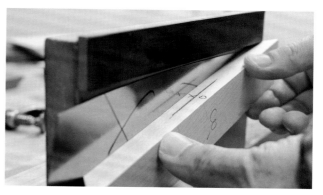

16 Make similar cuts in the lid. This time there will be an O visible in front of the spacer so we need to apply the rule: **'If you can see the area marked with an O, insert a saw blade spacer'.**

17 The depth stop remains in the same position to make these cuts.

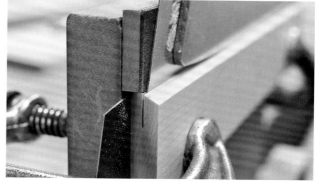

18 First, make a 10mm cut. Next, make a side cut to remove the unnecessary parts.

19 Place the rabbeting guide on its side, making sure the unwanted material is on top. Fix the wood with double-sided tape. Be careful – for this type of box, the unwanted lid and body parts are reversed.

20 Attach the 10.3mm spacer.

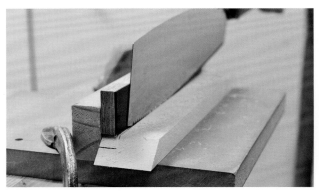

21 Carefully cut into the unwanted material. Be sure not to cut too deep.

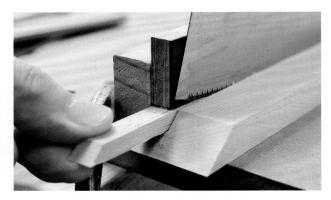

22 The unwanted part is cut, as shown.

23 Process all the lid materials in this way.

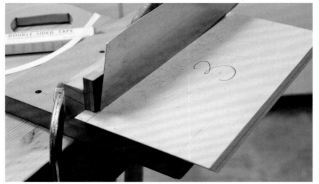

24 Similarly, we can now cut the body materials and remove the unwanted parts. First, check the Xs to see which part is unwanted and then set it on the jig. The unwanted parts will be reversed for the lid and body.

25 The unwanted part is now detached.

26 Risers and shoulders are complete.

27 When dry fitting be sure to closely check the rabbets. Here, they should be just a little tight. After gluing, the shoulders can be corrected with a planer.

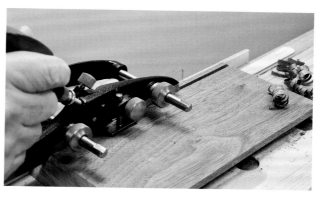

28 To insert the bottom board, groove the body with a 4mm groove planer. The depth should be 5mm (see step 5 on page 106).

29 Grooving the bottom plates is complete.

Grooving top boards

30 Groove the lid pieces. The top board is also made of 4mm plywood, so the groove planer blade width is 4mm. Once again, the depth is 5mm, same as the bottom board.

31 Top board grooving is now also complete.

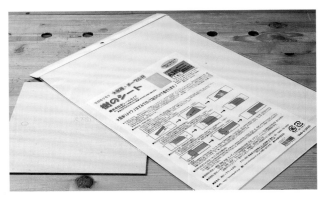

32 Cut out the top and bottom panels and attach a thin sheet of maple veneer (self-adhesive veneer). It should be about the size of a sheet of paper with adhesive on one side (see step 6 on page 106).

33 Peel off the backing paper on the veneer sheet, little-by-little, and stick it on the top board. The trick is to apply the sheet while forcing out the air.

34 After applying the maple veneer to the top board, it will be a little bit over 4mm thick. To make this thinner, I used a planer to cut around the top board's back side. Note that the planer blade is angled a little towards the outside.

35 To glue the lid and body together, place aluminium right-angle material at each of the four corners, tighten with a belt clamp and glue everything at the same time (see step 7 on page 106).

36 First, connect the materials by pulling them together and then masking. We will use these as 'hinges'.

37 Connect both the lid and body materials with masking tape, as shown.

38 For the lid, apply glue to the 45-degree corners. Insert the top board into the grooves as you join the materials together.

39 Glue the body in the same way as the lid.

40 Wrap a belt clamp around the aluminium right-angle material while holding the aluminium pieces against the corners. Before tightening, be sure to add the lid. To prevent the two pieces from sticking together, insert sticks as shown.

41 Tighten everything. Square all right angles and, when correcting, apply clamps on the diagonal. Tighten slightly. If the aluminium material is a little long, you can use a string on the diagonal instead of a clamp.

42 Here is a view of one of the sticks between the lid and the body.

43 As you can see this is quite a busy gluing process. However, if you prepare everything needed in advance, you won't have to panic.

Fixing with a planer

44 A shoulder plane was used to shave the riser rabbets, occasionally putting the lid on to check fit and to make adjustments. Since it is a perfectly square box, the lid can be put on in any position and checked for a smooth fit.

45 The bottom edge of the lid must also be flat.

46 The top of the lid must also be smoothly finished. The top surface seen here is the one we attached maple veneer to in step 33.

47 Here is the underside of the body. To make sure it won't rattle when it is on a flat surface, plane it flat.

48 Finish the upper edge of the risers as well. To prevent gaps between the lid and the body, we need to cut them a little more than necessary and make sure the risers are slightly low.

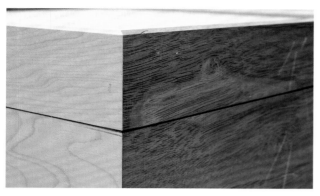

49 Here we see the box with the lid on. Closely examine the box perimeter – there are both wide and narrow gaps. By looking closely, you can determine exactly where to adjust with a plane.

50 Adjust the gap by cutting the shoulder on the body.

51 With the lid on, finish all four side panels with a planer.

52 The box is now complete, with a perfectly aligned lid.

LEVEL 3
BOX JOINT BASICS – FIVE INTERLOCKING PINS

The box joint is a strong and beautiful structure used for boxes and furniture. In this section, we will introduce the five interlocking pins box joint. This joint is most often divided into an odd number of pieces, such as three, five or seven.

The unique methods in this book use a tail guide and a saw blade spacer with bevel to make the process easier and more accurate. However, this is a difficult technique, so a certain amount of practice is required. Test cutting before the actual work is a good way to practise and to check the fit (tightness/looseness).

The reason why conventional methods are difficult is that the wood has to be freehand cut at right angles and the positioning is most often determined by eye. Here, right-angle cuts are left to the tail guide, while the cut position is determined by the saw blade spacer with bevel. This way, even beginners can perform the advanced cuts necessary for excellent box joints. Note that the saw blade spacer with bevel is a particularly important tool for determining cut positions, and key to making these joints, so it's important to perfectly understand how to use them. The tail guide and the saw blade spacer with bevel are shown on page 119.

FIVE INTERLOCKING PINS – BOX JOINT SEQUENCE DIAGRAM 1

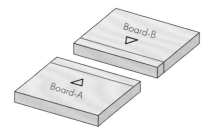

1 Mark the joint area on the front face with a triangle. Scribe the area to be cut to opposite board thickness. Note, the blue line in the illustration is scribed (see steps 2 and 3 on page 118).

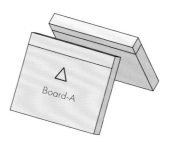

2 Lift the pieces so that they are folded up and back-to-back (see step 2 on page 118).

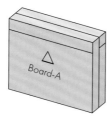

3 Align the reference line sides and fix in a bench vice (see step 4 on page 118).

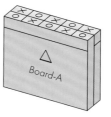

4 Divide the wood into five parts and scribe. Write Xs and Os on the sections, as shown. Note that both ends of Board-A are marked with Os (see step 4 on page 118).

MARKING

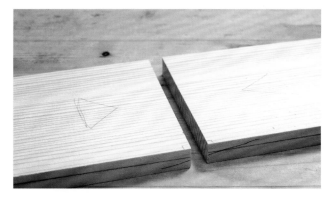

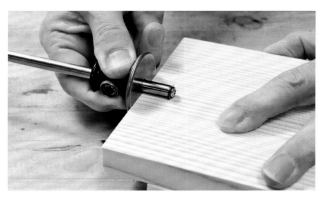

1 Prepare two pieces of wood. Decide which will be Board-A and Board-B. The thick line in the photo is the datum line (see step 2 on page 117). Mark the board face with a triangle (see step 1 on page 117).

2 Set the marking gauge and scribe the back of the target piece. This is called the baseline. The front side is ruled with a pencil so it can be erased. The thick part of Board-B is also scribed. This line marks the bottom cut line (shown in steps 1 and 2 on page 117).

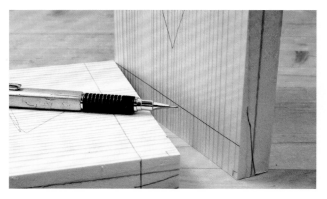

3 Use a pencil to mark the front side. Use the opposite piece to mark the precise thickness.

4 Align the datum lines and clamp the pieces together. Divide the board widthwise into five sections and scribe them with a square and utility knife (see steps 3 and 4 on page 117).

5 After dividing, mark Xs and Os in alternating blocks. Make sure Board-B (which also has scribed lines on the thick part) has an X on each end. Now, each piece can be processed separately.

PROCESSING

We will cut only the left sides of O marks, in turn. Place the saw blade spacer with bevel on the scribed line so that the O mark on the spacer and the O mark on the wood piece face each other. This is where we need to cut. Place the tail guide over the saw blade spacer to keep it upright as you cut.

FIVE INTERLOCKING PINS – BOX JOINT SEQUENCE DIAGRAM 2

1 Cut along the solid red lines on the left side of the Os. For dotted lines, turn the material around and cut (see step 1 on page 120).

2 Place the saw blade spacer with bevel on the scribed line, with Os facing each other (see step 2 on page 120).

3 Place the tail guide up against the saw blade spacer with bevel (see step 3 on page 120).

4 Remove the spacer, while firmly holding the tail guide (see step 4 on page 120).

Straight-toothed, flush-cut saw

5 Place the saw against the tail guide's magnetic sheet and cut (see step 5 on page 120).

6 The first cut has been made. Next, cut along the solid line on the left (see step 6 on page 120).

7 Set the saw blade spacer with bevel on the solid line and butt the tail guide up against it (see step 7 on page 121).

8 Remove the saw blade spacer and place the saw against the guide to cut (see step 8 on page 121).

9 Next, turn the material around and cut along the dotted lines. When you turn the piece around, the dotted lines will be left of the Os (see step 10 on page 121).

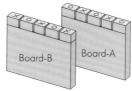
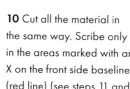

10 Cut all the material in the same way. Scribe only in the areas marked with an X on the front side baseline (red line) (see steps 11 and 12 on page 121).

HOW TO MAKE A FIVE INTERLOCKING PINS BOX JOINT

1 Let's start processing from here. Cut left of the Os, as indicated by solid red lines. After that, turn the material around and cut dotted lines. When you turn it around, the dotted lines will be left of the Os (see step 1 on page 119).

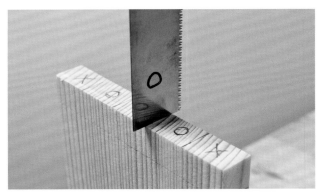

2 Place the sharp edge of the saw blade spacer with bevel on the scribed line, left of the O. Make sure the material O and the saw blade spacer O face each other. Be careful not to place the saw blade spacer in the wrong direction (see step 2 on page 119).

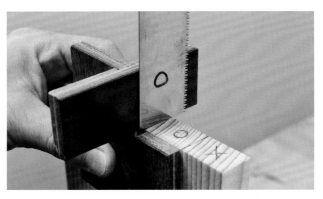

3 Butt the tail guide up against the saw blade spacer until it connects with the magnetic sheet. The tail guide makes the saw blade spacer stand upright (see step 3 on page 119).

4 Hold the tail guide firmly in place and remove the saw blade spacer. The magnetic sheet surface is positioned at a distance equal to the thickness of the saw blade spacer with bevel from the scribed line (see step 4 on page 119).

5 Affix the brass depth stop to the saw blade and cut (see step 5 on page 119).

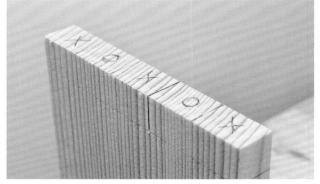

6 The incision has been made. The next step is to cut the left side of the other O (see step 6 on page 119).

7 Set up the saw blade spacer with bevel the same as before. Position the tail guide (see step 7 on page 119).

8 Remove the spacer and cut (see step 8 on page 119).

9 The first two cuts have been made.

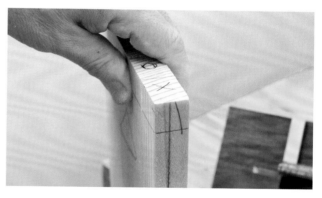

10 Flip the piece around. This is how we will cut the dotted line from step 1 on page 120. Once flipped, the dotted line will be left of the O (see step 9 on page 119).

11 Make an incision left of the O mark. Following the above steps we can make cuts at all points of both Board-A and Board-B (see step 10 on page 119).

12 The baselines on both Board-A and Board-B can now be scribed. Only sections marked with Xs should be scribed. This photo shows Board-A (see step 10 on page 119).

CUTTING OFF BOTH ENDS OF BOARD-B

Once you have finished cutting into both the Board-A and Board-B end grain, cut off the ends of Board-B.

FIVE INTERLOCKING PINS – BOX JOINT SEQUENCE DIAGRAM 3

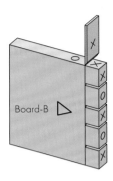

1 Cut off both ends. This time, align the X mark on the saw blade spacer with bevel with the X mark on the wood (see step 2 opposite).

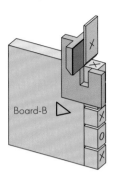

2 Place the tail guide up against the saw blade spacer with bevel (see step 2 opposite).

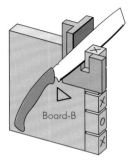

3 Remove spacer and cut vertically (see step 3 opposite).

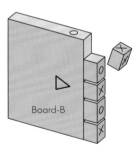

4 The unnecessary part has been removed. Cut off the remaining end (see step 4 opposite).

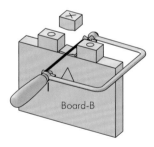

5 Cut near the baseline with a coping saw (see step 6 opposite).

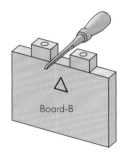

6 Finish with a chisel. Finish all cuts this way (see step 9 on page 124).

HOW TO CUT OFF BOTH ENDS OF BOARD-B

1 Since both ends of Board-B are marked with Xs, they need to be cut off with the tail guide.

2 Set up the saw blade spacer with bevel and attach the tail guide to it, paying particular attention to the spacer direction. Butt the spacer up against the X-marked tail guide (shown in steps 1 and 2 opposite).

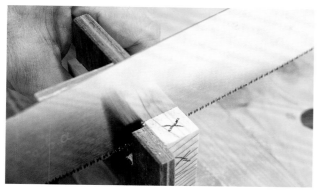

3 Remove spacer and cut. Remove the part marked with an X (see step 3 opposite).

4 The X part has been removed (see step 4 opposite).

5 Both ends of Board-B have been cut off.

6 Use a coping saw to roughly cut out the remaining X (see step 5 opposite).

7 Board-A can now be processed in the same way.

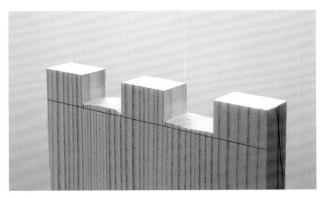

8 You can see that the cuts are near the baseline, not on or below it!

9 Shave off 1mm at a time with a chisel. If the blade is placed directly on the baseline, the wedge effect will cause it to be pushed over the line. Chisel down to half the thickness, flip it over and finish from the other side (see step 6 on page 122).

10 Finally, place the chisel edge vertically on the baseline and cut about 2mm. Now, tilt the chisel slightly inwards and cut halfway. Flip the piece over and finish in the same way. In this way, the bottom will have a slight V-shape.

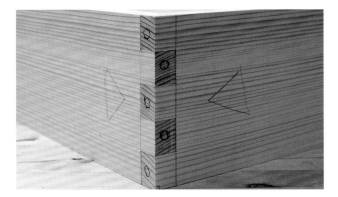

11 Here it is, assembled and finished.

SAW BLADE SPACER WITH BEVEL AND VINYL TAPE

In my experience, I have found that using a saw blade spacer with bevel without sharpening can create a loose fit. To make a tighter fit, however, you can adjust the thickness of the tape. For now, apply a layer of vinyl tape about 0.3mm thick to the X side of the saw blade spacer. Different people have different habits when they scribe and cut, so you should play around until you find the right thickness of vinyl tape for your style.

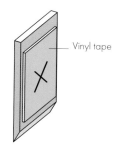

Adjust fit by applying 0.3mm vinyl tape on X marked surface.

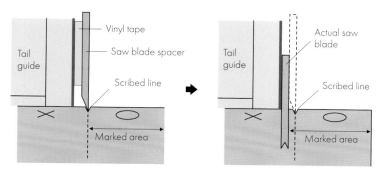

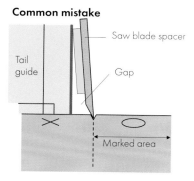

When vinyl tape is applied to the saw blade spacer, the tail guide will recede by that amount, allowing for a wider cut in the O marked area.

Remove the saw blade spacer and cut with a raw blade to widen one side of the O-marked area by the thickness of the vinyl tape. This will tighten the assembly.

If the tail guide isn't tightly aligned with the spacer, a gap will be created. This will lead to misaligned cuts.

ADJUSTING THE FIT

You can make your own simple chisel guide with these steps.

This guide is placed over the top of the target area and you cut in from the pin side of the end grain.

Looking up from below, you can see that the chisel cuts while the guide is held tightly against pins. The chisel blade back (flat surface) is placed firmly against the guide.

LEVEL 4
BOX JOINT THAT HIDES BOTTOM BOARD RABBETS

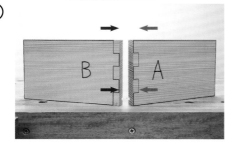

In 'Level 3: box joint basics', we learned how to make standard box joints (1). However, when making an actual box we need to add a floor plate. For this, we will groove the inside of the box bottom. This can be done with a groove planer, but the groove will travel from one end of your target piece to the other (groove) (2). This will inevitably cause the end of the groove to be visible from outside the box (3).

To solve this problem, both ends of the groove can be removed by rabbeting. Now, the joint can be made without a visible groove (4). Photo 5 shows two boards that have already been grooved. The top and bottom ends of Board-A aren't cut off. Instead, they are left as pins (red arrows). On the other hand, the top and bottom ends of Board-B are cut off (blue arrows). When performing this process, Board-A is rabbeted first, then Board-B.

Here we will use a temporary saw guide made of L-shaped aluminium angle material (cross-sectional dimensions of about 20 x 20 x 3mm) with a magnetic sheet attached to one side.

126

GROOVE DEPTH AND SPACER THICKNESS

Groove depth

Depth stop

Spacer

When hiding floor plate grooves, the relationship between groove depth and rabbet depth is paramount. Determine the spacer thickness and groove depth before beginning. Just make sure the rabbeting depth is slightly larger than the groove depth – as shown in step 4 on page 128. In this case, the spacer thickness is 5.2mm, so the groove depth is set to 5mm. Rabbeting is performed with a rabbeting guide.

HOW TO MAKE A BOX JOINT THAT HIDES BOTTOM BOARD RABBETS

Rabbeting Board-A

1 Cut a groove in for the floor plate. The groove planer should set the groove depth to a value that is less than the spacer thickness. In this case, the depth is 5mm.

2 Put the two pieces of wood together and divide into five sections. Use a cutter, or a similar tool, to scribe. Next, mark Xs and Os. Notice that both ends of Board-A are marked with Os – in this photo, Board-A is in front.

3 Start with Board-A. Attach the spacer to the rabbeting guide and clamp to the material. The thickness of the spacer is 5.2mm, and cut depth is equal to the material thickness.

4 Attach a depth stop to the saw blade to cut the correct thickness. The rabbet is 5.8mm, which is the sum of the spacer thickness (5.2mm) and the saw blade thickness (0.6mm).

5 After ripping is complete, we must decide where to cut off the rabbet. Lay Board-A on its side against a piece of scrap. Using Board-B as a spacer, attach the temporary saw guide with double-sided tape while butting it up against Board-B.

6 Carefully remove unnecessary parts. This eliminates the groove in the area to be glued.

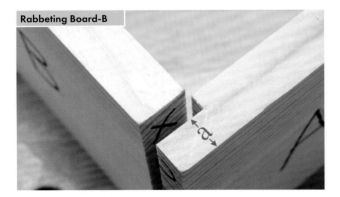

Rabbeting Board-B

7 Board-B also needs to be rabbeted. Even without rabbeting, the groove will be hidden by the Board-A piece, but the edge thickness will be different. Note that the thickness of 'a' (see photo) must be the cut depth for Board-B.

8 Use the 'a' section as a guide when affixing your depth stop.

9 Cut with the rabbeting guide as usual.

10 Clamp Board-B against a scrap piece of wood. Be sure to use the rabbet of Board-A as a spacer. Attach a temporary sawing guide with double-sided tape, as shown.

11 Cut off the rabbet.

12 Board-A and Board-B have been rabbeted, as seen in the photo. The next step is to make the joint. The thickness of 'b' (see photo) is the cut depth of Board-A.

13 First, Board-A. Use the marking gauge to scribe lines at the base of each X slot. This is where the chisel will be placed to carve out the recess. Lines must be scribed on both sides.

14 Roughly cut with a coping saw and finish with a chisel.

CHISELLING A JOINT WITHOUT A RABBET

When chiselling a joint without a rabbet, we place the target board directly on the bench and chisel it as shown in the photo, below left. For a joint with a rabbet, as in this case, we use a cut-off to support the joint (photo, below right).

15 Cut in from the end grain of Board-B. The cut depth should match the rabbeted area. Align the gauge with the edge of Board-B and the rabbeted section. Mark only the front side of the X sections. Board-B is then finished in the same way as Board-A.

16 Dry fit. Once assembled you will note that the floor plate groove is no longer visible from the outside.

17 On the left is our joint with the hidden floor plate groove. On the right shows a simple joint without any groove. Although they are made from the same thickness of wood, you can see that the left pins are thinner due to rabbeting.

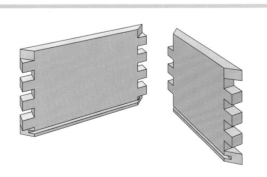

As far as hiding rabbets goes, in addition to our 'Box joint that hides bottom board rabbets' method, there is a separate technique that uses mitred ends, as shown in the figure above.

LEVEL 5
RABBET JOINT BOX

This box is made with standard rabbet joints, while the lid and body are fitted together using *Hon-Inro* (risers and shoulders). This is distinguished from *Tsuke-Inro*, which uses separate plates for the risers and shoulders to create a tiered shape.

This section is explained by machining only one corner, not the entire box. In addition to the ripping guide and cross-cut guide, the rabbeting

guide will be used. You will also need spacers that are about half the material thickness.

In this case, the material is 19mm, so I used 10.3mm spacers, which is close enough to half the material thickness. Processing the risers and shoulders is basically the same as for the half lap joint (see page 42). The rule of: 'If you can see the area marked with an O, insert a saw blade spacer' applies here as well.

RABBET JOINT BOX SEQUENCE DIAGRAM

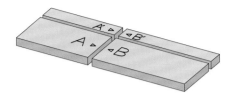

1 Cut Boards-A and A′ and Boards-B and B′ (see step 2 opposite).

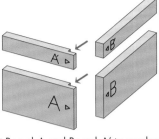

2 Rabbet Board-A and Board-A′ to produce the half lap joint (see arrow). Don't forget to insert a saw blade spacer in the rabbeting guide (see step 6 opposite).

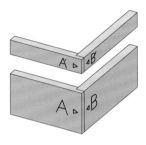

3 Dry fit and check (see step 11 on page 134).

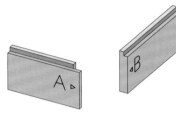

4 Rabbet the risers on Board-A and Board-B (see step 12 on page 134).

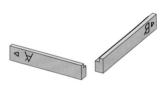

5 Rabbet the shoulders on Board-A′ and Board-B′. Insert the saw blade spacer in the rabbeting guide (see step 15 on page 135).

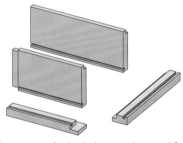

6 Make grooves for both the top plate and floor plate (see step 25 on page 137).

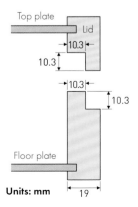

Top plate

Lid

10.3

10.3

10.3

10.3

Floor plate

Units: mm

19

HOW TO MAKE A RABBET JOINT BOX

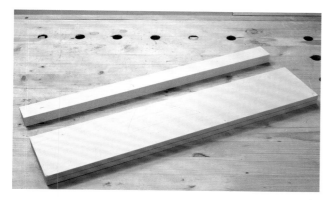

1 Here are the lid and body pieces. Instead of cutting the finished box into a separate lid and body, we process the cut pieces from the beginning.

2 Cut two sets for the lid: Boards-A and B and Boards-A' and B'. The sides to be joined are marked with a triangle. The half lap joint rabbet is made along the edge of Board-A. The sides in the photo make up the outside (front) of the box (see step 1 opposite).

3 Boards-A and B are stood up and a spacer is placed on them. The spacer divides the rabbeting area in two parts, as shown. The parts marked with an X are cut off for the rabbets. This photo shows the body, so the outside will be rabbeted.

4 The same spacer has now been placed on the lid material. Note, the lid material is flipped over here. The tool used to make the rabbets is a rabbeting guide.

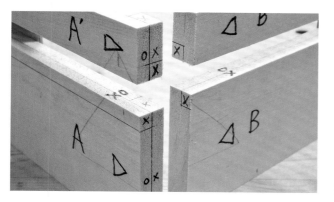

5 The photo shows the lid and body with Xs, Os and rabbet lines drawn on them. Rabbets are made at the X marks on Boards-A and A', NOT on the edge of the Boards-B and B'.

6 Attach a 10.3mm spacer to the rabbeting guide (or ripping guide) and clamp a box piece with the front side facing out. Don't forget the rule of: **'If you can see the area marked with an O, insert a saw blade spacer'.** The cut depth is the thickness of the B material (see step 2 opposite).

7 The next step is to clamp the wood to the cross-cut guide to cut off the X-marked area. You can see that the material thickness is the actual thickness of A'.

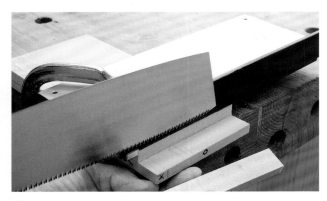

8 The X-marked area has been cleanly cut.

9 Clamp Board-A' to the rabbeting guide, marked side facing out. Cut.

10 Using the cross-cut guide, cut off the unnecessary X-marked part. See step 8.

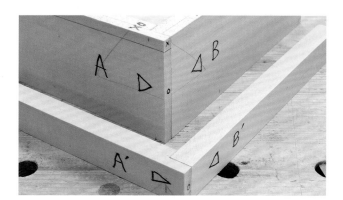

11 Here is the dry fit. After this, the rabbets will be cut out (see step 3 on page 132).

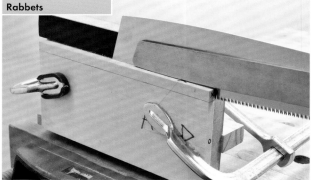

Rabbets

12 Use the rabbeting guide on Board-A. Again, clamp with the outside facing out. The saw blade spacer isn't used because the X is visible in this instance. Set the cut depth to 10.3mm and cut (see step 4 on page 132).

13 Make a similar cut in Board-B. It's longer than the guide, so clamp it with the front (heel end) overhanging the guide a little. Cut from the back (left end of Board-B). Don't try to cut all the way through, cut halfway through on the first pass.

14 Shift the material and re-clamp. Now, cut the front section and you're done.

15 Board-A' (which will form the lid) is cut in the same way. However, as you can see, the O is in front of the spacer, so we need to add a saw blade spacer (see step 5 on page 132).

16 Cut with the depth stop set to 10.3mm.

17 Cut Board-B' in the same way, with a saw blade spacer, and at a depth of 10.3mm. Board-B' is quite long so it needs an overhang at the front (the heel). Be sure to clamp before starting to cut.

18 Complete by shifting the piece and cutting the front section.

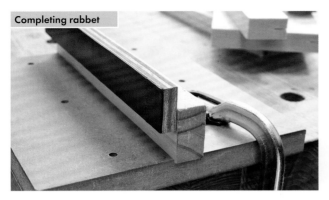

19 Remove the 10.3mm spacer. Clamp the rabbeting guide sideways on the workbench. As you can see in the photo, it's better to make the work surface a little wider so that the entire spacer can be stabilized. See 'Rabbeting guide' on page 186.

20 Place the material under the spacer and clamp. You can cut off the X-marked wood at the 10.3mm position and make a rabbet. To be precise, cut 10.3mm + 0.6mm of saw blade thickness. However, you can correct the 0.6mm with a planer later.

21 Cut off the X portion and remove it.

22 Here are the rabbeted pieces.

23 Here are the pieces once they have been dry fit.

24 You can clearly see the half lap joint construction here.

Grooving for top plate and floor plate

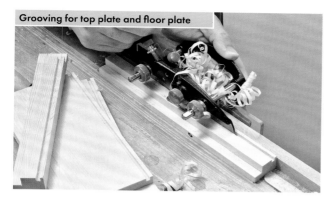

25 Make a groove for fitting the top plate in the lid and for fitting the floor plate in the body (see step 6 on page 132).

Gluing

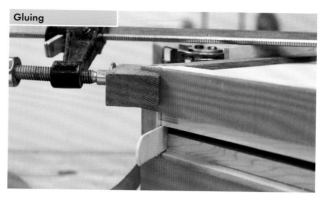

26 Use the aluminium angle material for the corners. Glue the lid and body at the same time. See steps 35 to 43 on pages 112–114 for reference.

LEVEL 6
FINGER-JOINTED BOX WITH LID

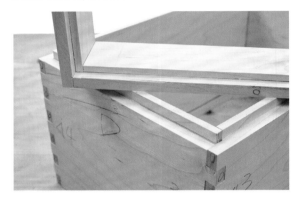

Lid risers and body shoulders

When making a finger-jointed box with lid, a spacer about half the material thickness is used to cut the risers and shoulders. The same spacer is used for rabbeting the box joints as well.

The floor depth and top plate grooves should be less than the spacer thickness. For example, for a 10mm thick piece of wood, the spacer thickness should be 5mm. This will result in the lid shoulders and the body risers also being 5mm. In addition, the rabbet depth at both ends of Board-A will be 5mm. The floor plate groove depth and Board-B should be less than 5mm. In other words, the spacer thickness you select

will affect the riser and shoulder depths, the rabbet depth on both boards and the groove depth for the floor plate.

In reality, it is difficult to find spacers that are exactly 5mm thick, so 4mm or 6mm is fine. If you choose a 4mm spacer, the bottom plate groove should be less than 4mm. If you choose a 6mm spacer, the groove should be less than 6mm.

A tail guide and saw blade spacer with bevel are used for the box joint. We will also use a coping saw, chisel, groove planer, fine drill bit and router bit.

RISERS, SHOULDERS AND CUTTING DIMENSIONS

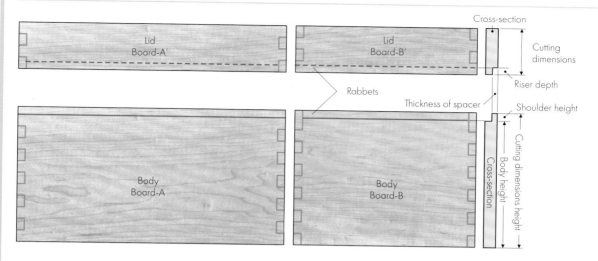

Prepare the lid and body pieces in advance. Divide the body height into an odd number of sections and mark out finger joints. The body height is calculated by adding the shoulder height (about 10mm) to the body height. The riser section's front side will be rabbeted later.

The lid height (meaning the width of the lid material) is also divided into sections and processed into finger joints. There is no need to add the shoulder height to cut the wood. The finger joints on the lid should be made to match the finger joints on the body. Map things out and decide on finger joint size and number accordingly.

RABBET DEPTH AND BOX JOINT PROCESSING (VIEWED FROM ABOVE)

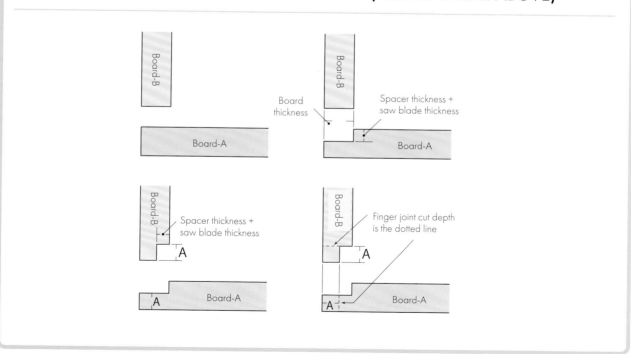

FINGER-JOINTED BOX WITH LID SEQUENCE DIAGRAM

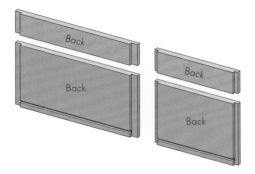

1 These boards have been grooved, to accommodate the bottom plate, and rabbeted at both ends (see step 1 opposite).

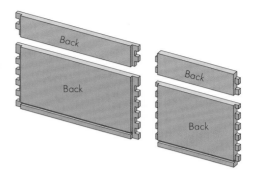

2 Process the finger joints on the rabbeted sections (see step 2 opposite).

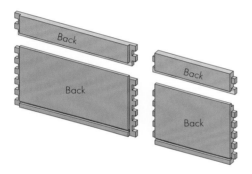

3 Process the shoulders and risers (see step 11 on page 142)

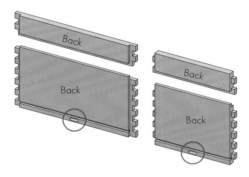

4 Make an elongated hole for string in the bottom of the body (see step 21 on page 144).

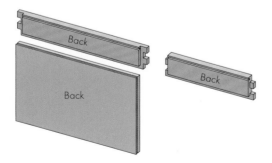

5 Cut grooves in the lid frame to house the top plate (see step 25 on page 145).

HOW TO MAKE A FINGER-JOINTED BOX WITH LID

1 Rabbet both ends of the lid and body pieces. Grooves for housing floor plates are within the rabbet cuts. See page 125 for work done up to this point. Cut the wood with the front side facing outwards, clamped to the rabbeting guide (see step 1 opposite).

2 Clamp together the ends to be joined and scribe the lines for finger joints. To prevent the two pieces from shifting, insert a perfectly fit square dowel into the corresponding groove, as shown (see step 2 opposite).

3 We cut finger joints one board at a time. You can tell this is Board-A because it starts with an O.

4 Use a coping saw to cut off unwanted parts close to the baseline.

5 Finish baseline sections with a chisel. The ends are rabbeted, so we need to chisel while using a piece of scrap as a support. This will prevent chipping of the finger joint baseline.

6 Scribe finger joint divisions on the lid pieces. You can tell by the rabbet depths that the left side is Board-B' and the right is Board-A' (see page 117).

7 Use the coping saw to roughly cut out unnecessary parts.

8 Put everything together for a dry fit.

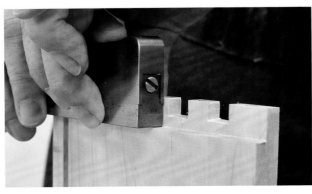

9 If necessary, use a planer to modify fit.

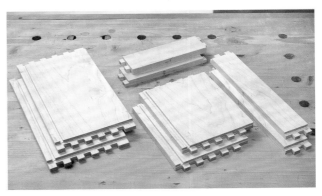

10 All parts have now been processed.

Processing risers and shoulders

11 Clamp the material to the rabbeting guide, front side facing out. The photo shows a piece of lid material. We need to insert a spacer, as shown, to follow our rule: '**If you can see the area marked with an O, insert a saw blade spacer**' (see step 3 on page 140).

12 Attach a depth stop at 8mm to cut riser to height.

13 Material should be shifted and re-clamped after first cut because it is longer than the rabbeting guide.

14 Cut the body piece in the same manner. We see an X in front of the cutting spacer, so there is no need for a saw blade spacer.

15 Cut to 8mm as set by the depth stop. Process all body pieces.

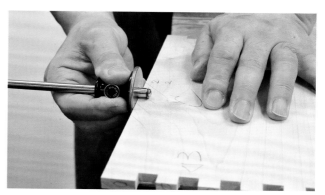

16 This process is for marking out the rabbet. Scribe lines 8mm in from the material edge.

17 Attach a magnetic sheet to a guide made of square aluminium or L-shaped angle material. Attach double-sided tape to the bottom of the guide. Attach two large utility knife blades to the aluminium guide and then place the knife blades on the scribed lines, as shown.

18 Remove the utility knife blades and then cut off unnecessary parts.

19 Cut off all unnecessary parts.

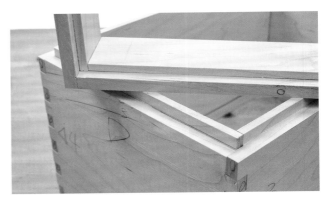

20 Dry fit again. Notice that the risers and shoulders are now complete.

Elongated hole for threading string

21 To make several elongated holes using a drill press, first push the pieces firmly against the fence, also attaching stoppers, as shown. Even if the material moves left or right, it will stop before moving past the end holes (see step 4 on page 140).

22 Drill left and right end-holes first. Then drill between them, like making stepping stones. The drill bit is 2.5mm thick.

23 Once the holes are drilled, replace that bit with a thin router bit and gradually work the hole deeper and deeper, while moving the material from side to side. The bit used here is a 3.2mm down-cut spiral bit.

Processing top panel

24 If the top plate edges are not trimmed at right angles, correct them with an edge plane or a shooting board.

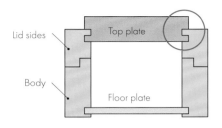

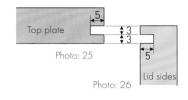

Lid sides

Top plate

Body

Floor plate

5

3
3

Top plate

Photo: 25

Photo: 26

5

Lid sides

Units: mm

LID FRAME GROOVING

This diagram shows how the top plate and lid frame are joined. The top plate can be attached using a variety of methods, including simply gluing it on. However, in this section we will show you how to house the top plate inside the lid frame itself. If a 3mm blade is attached to the groove planer and the planer fence is set to the same distance of 3mm, both the top plate and the lid frame can be processed with the same settings. This is a very convenient woodworking technique.

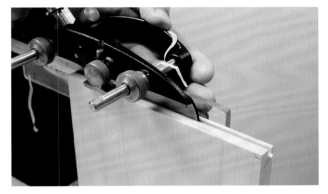

25 Cut grooves all the way around the top plate. Set the groove depth to 5mm and work in this order: edge, end grain, edge and end grain. Here, there's a chip on the right end of edge, this will disappear once finished (see step 5 on page 140).

26 The processing of the top plate is complete when we have cut all the way around to the beginning of the starting point.

27 Grooving the lid material. The fence distance and depth settings remain the same.

28 Grooving on all top plates and lid materials is complete. In the photo, you can see a small gap on the right end. This will disappear once the pieces are pushed together tightly.

29 Dry fit the lid and check everything. Glue the lid and body together at the same time.

30 Place the aluminium angle material on the corners and tighten with belt clamps. Attach a thin rubber sheet to the inside of the angle material with masking tape. The sheet ensures that finger joints are pressed firmly into place.

31 Square dowels are placed between the lid and the body, so that any leaking glue won't accidentally glue the pieces together.

32 The entire piece is finished by planing.

LEVEL 7
FRAME AND PANEL JOINT BOX

Frame and panel joint boxes make convenient use of the grooves made for fitting panels (or mitred inset panels) into the stile and rail framing. This style of box is also more economical as it is made with plywood panels and frames, rather than solid panelling.

In this section, we will only discuss the main structure and reinforcement points. The new-type vertical ripping guide is used for cutting the 'tenons' (tongues in this case) that fit into the grooves. For more information about this guide, please see page 18.

The overall structure is completed by first making the four frames – front, back, left and right – and then assembling them.

Structural drawing

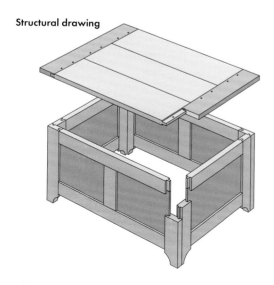

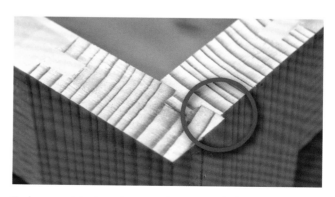

The frames are joined together in a similar manner to the frame and panel joint method described previously. Gaps are made between the frames, which are later corrected with a planer.

HOW TO MAKE A FRAME AND PANEL JOINT BOX

1 Long pieces are grooved before cutting out the individual members. The grooves don't have to be in the exact centre. After grooving, cut to the required length.

2 The 'tenons' on both ends are cut with the new-type vertical ripping guide. These are not proper tenons, but more like end tongues. The tongues should be cut out slightly thicker than necessary. Their depth is the same as the groove depth.

3 Use a planer to thin the tongues until they fit perfectly.

FRAME AND PANEL JOINT REINFORCING – PART 1

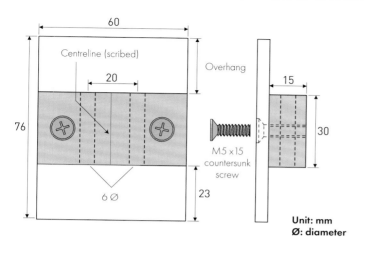

Centreline (scribed)

60

20

76

6 Ø

23

Overhang

15

30

M5 x 15 countersunk screw

Unit: mm
Ø: diameter

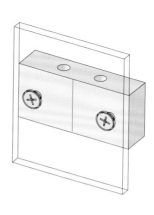

1 One of the weaknesses of frame and panel joints is that the amount of material between the groove and tongue is limited. Reinforcing with dowels is easy and effective.

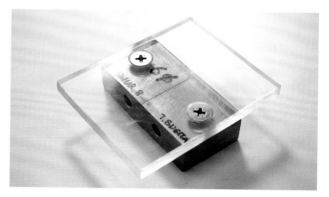

2 This is a custom dowel hole jig.

3 Mark the joint with a pencil line, as shown. Drill dowel holes in both end grain and wood edge, without turning the dowel hole jig around. If you don't make adjustments, the holes will be shallower than the grooves and tongues. That being said, make sure to adjust the depth of your drill and make the holes as deep as possible.

FRAME AND PANEL JOINT REINFORCING – PART 2

1 When using this joint to make side panels for large storage boxes or cabinets, the joint can be reinforced with actual tenons. In this case, it is common to process the groove width according to the panel thickness and drill mortices that are the same size as the groove width. Grooves are cut with a groove planer, and holes are drilled with the dowel hole jig mounted on a drill press. We assumed 9mm plywood panels would be used here, so we have used 9mm for both the groove planer blade width and the drill bit thickness. When actually producing boxes or cabinets, just change the blade and bit sizes to match your target panel thickness.

2 Find and mark the position of the mortice hole. Here, there are small blocks attached to both ends of the holes with double-sided tape. By simply placing the drill bit here, the position of the holes at both ends can be accurately determined.

3 First, drill holes at both ends. Then, drill the 'stepping stone' holes. Connect the holes. Finally, press the material firmly against the fence and move it from side to side to flatten the walls. For more information, see 'Mortice jig' on page 231.

4 Mortice holes aren't centred in the pieces, so you will need to note the distance of each tenon from the edge. This distance will be the spaces thickness inserted into the new-type vertical ripping guide.

5 Install a 9mm blade into the groove planer. Let the blade protrude about 10mm.

6 Insert the 9mm blade into the mortice hole made with a 9mm drill bit. It should fit perfectly without any gaps.

7 Attach the groove planer, with the fence in the shown position, and place it against the wood. The distance from the fence to the groove is now exactly the same as the tenon hole in the fence. This set is complete.

8 Return the groove planer back to its original state and start grooving.

9 All materials are now grooved and morticed.

Tenon processing

10 Insert a spacer of the same thickness as the target groove wall into the new-type vertical ripping guide and rip vertically. The rule of: **'If you can see the area marked with an O, insert a saw blade spacer'** applies here.

11 Make 5mm cuts at both ends of the tenon.

12 Use the cross-cut guide to cut off unwanted parts at the proper tenon length.

13 Leave the convex bulge on top of the piece so that the groove will be hidden when assembled.

14 This completes most of the processing.

15 Flip the piece over and chamfer the bottom corners of the tenon holes with a box cutter.

16 Tenon joint reinforcement is complete.

LEVEL 8
DRAWERS

Since there are many different frames for drawers, I think that we should all be free to create our own. Here I will introduce some frames I usually make. The key is that any frame should fit snugly into its opening. To create an excellent fit, the side and front panels must first fit snugly into their respective opening. After gluing, drawers that are too snug to fit can be adjusted with a planer and finished so that they fit perfectly.

Make front and side panels using rabbet joints. See pages 100–104 for more information on rabbet joint processing. The floor panel is inserted into the groove from the back side, so the bottom edge of the rear panel only extends as far as the floor panel (see step 7 on page 154). In the structural drawing, the upper edge of the rear panel is a few mm lower than the side panels. However, it can be made flush with the side panels as well. Lowering the top edge by a few millimetres prevents it from snagging when pulling out the drawer if it's part of a chest of drawers. The top part is adjusted based on the bottom of the drawer above. Lay out the left and right boards by paying attention to their grain direction, as they will be planed from front to back in later modification.

Structural drawing

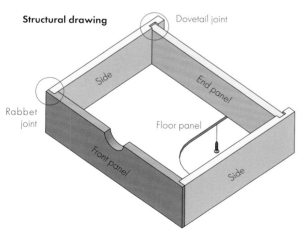

Dovetail joint

Side

End panel

Rabbet joint

Floor panel

Front panel

Side

DRAWER PRODUCTION SEQUENCE

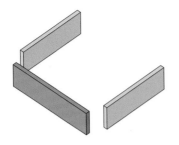

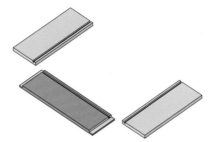

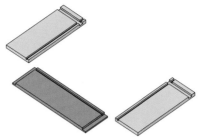

1 Adjust the side and front panels with a planer so that they just barely fill the drawer opening (see step 1 opposite).

2 Process the floor panel groove. Rabbet both ends of the front panel (see step 3 opposite).

3 Cut grooves in the side panels for receiving the end panel (see step 4 opposite).

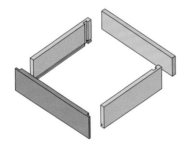

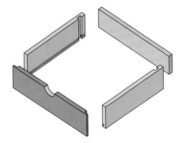

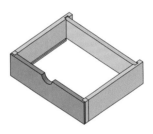

4 Cut out the end panel (see step 21 on page 158).

5 Cut the finger insertion area into the front panel (see step 23 on page 158).

6 Glue everything in place. Adjust with a planer so that it fits snugly into the opening (see step 24 on page 158).

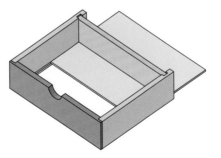

7 Cut out the floor panel and slide it into the grooves. Attach the floor panel to the end panel with wood screws.

HOW TO MAKE A DRAWER

1 Adjust the height of the side panels with a shooting board so they fit through their openings without gaps. If wood needs to be slightly tapered to fit, so be it. Cut the side panels a little longer and adjust them later (see step 1 opposite).

2 The front panels also need to be adjusted to fit their openings perfectly. In extreme cases, even if the opening is trapezoidal, just modify with a planer to fit the shape. Finish the drawers with a planer after fitting is complete.

3 The front panels are now in place, without any gaps. Next, both ends of the front panel are rabbeted. In addition, grooves in the front and side panels for inserting the floor panel are cut (see step 2 opposite).

Grooving to fit end panel

4 Cut a groove for inserting the end panel about 10 to 15mm from the rear end of each side plate. Use the Accurate Guide here (see step 3 opposite).

5 This is preliminary preparation for precisely setting the accurate guide. Determine the position using a ruler and square. Both side panels are positioned at right angles to the bottom edge for grooving.

6 Attach a craft stick with double-sided tape.

7 Attach the Accurate Guide to the material with double-sided tape. Make sure it rests against the craft stick. The Accurate Guide has a spacer sandwiched in it that is the same thickness as the saw blade.

8 Attach the depth stop to the saw blade and cut.

9 Remove the spacer from the Accurate Guide and insert a scrap piece of end panel instead. The groove width is now set.

10 With that in place, make the second cut.

11 Remove the Accurate Guide and make several cuts. This will make it easier to break up the unwanted portion of the groove.

12 Similarly, cut the other side panel with your Accurate Guide.

13 Use a scraper to pop out the unwanted portions of the groove. Just insert the scraper and tilt it, or twist it, inwards.

14 Here is the finished state. It's easier to break the pieces out, rather than chiselling them out.

15 Finish the groove to the correct depth with a router plane. Back off the depth a tiny bit when cutting the front.

16 The end panel should fit perfectly in the groove. You can eliminate saw streaks by lowering the router plane blade a little more or by making the cut depth of the saw shallower by about 0.5mm.

Determine drawer depth

17 Put the side panels and front panels into the drawer opening to dry fit. The drawer length (depth) can be adjusted by trimming the front edge of the side panels, since the grooving of the end panel has already been done.

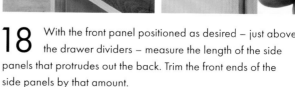

18 With the front panel positioned as desired – just above the drawer dividers – measure the length of the side panels that protrudes out the back. Trim the front ends of the side panels by that amount.

19 Here are the completed front and side panels. The next step is to cut out the end panels. I will explain how to determine their length.

20 Place the front panel on top of the side panel, near the rear grooves.

21 Measure the distance from groove to groove and cut out the end panel to that dimension. It's possible to shorten this length by about 1mm (see step 4 on page 154).

22 Tentatively assemble and check everything for a proper fit. Modify if necessary

23 Cut the hole (hook) for your fingers in the front panel. To prevent the wood from shifting, fix it firmly in place with stoppers and clamp. A forstner bit is being used in the photo (see step 5 on page 154).

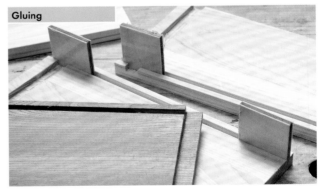

Gluing

24 Insert slightly tight pieces of scrap wood into the grooves to test bottom plate fit. This is to ensure that each component fits correctly (see step 6 on page 154).

25 Glue everything together. Clamp the side panels with a thick piece of scrap wood underneath to flush up the bottom. Use a bench vice to hold the drawer in place – front to back – and custom clamps to tighten side to side.

26 Plane the drawers as necessary to make sure they fit perfectly.

27 The planing is performed from front to back. The wood was selected so that the side panel grain would be pointing forwards.

Chapter 4
GUIDES AND JIGS

A guide or jig is an item used to control the movement of a tool, like a saw, to improve cutting accuracy. For example, if you want to cut a piece of wood at 45 degrees to make a picture frame, free handing will usually lead to angles that are off. This is precisely why we use some kind of tool – to cut accurately! The unique methods in this book are based on the use of a variety of such guides and jigs, and it allows even beginners to perform advanced joint processing with relative ease. And don't worry. After you make and use your first guide or jig, you'll definitely find ways to improve it. Then, when you make a second one, you'll notice significant improvement. By your third one, you'll find yourself producing perfectly functional jigs and guides.

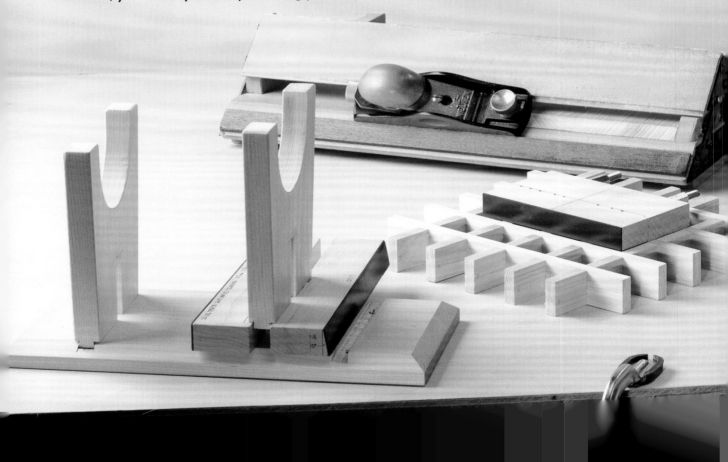

SHOOTING BOARD
AND BENCH HOOK

There are several types of shooting boards. Here, we'll introduce
you to one that is used to shave down edges with a shooting plane.

BENCH HOOK

1 The photo shows a box being finished with a planer. You can see a small piece of wood glued to the underside to make the 'cleat' part of the bench hook that butts up against the workbench. Note that there is also an adjustable fence on top of the bench hook. If your piece is placed against the fence, it won't move and can be easily worked.

2 The fence position has been changed so that a slightly longer piece of wood can be planed. The thinner the fence in this case, the better. If the fence is too thick, you won't be able to plane thin pieces of wood. As you can see, the fence in the photo is movable. It is made from a 5mm thick aluminium plate with holes drilled through it. Please note that the aluminium plate is covered with a thin wooden board so that the screw heads won't come in direct contact with the planer blade.

3 The back side is machined to create long countersunk holes. The metal parts are called weld nuts.

4 If you are planing small pieces, a small bench cleat will be easier to use.

SHOOTING BOARD

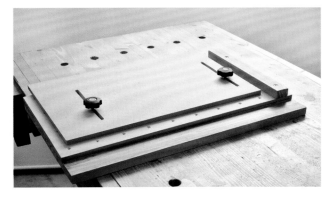

1 This is a planer board for finishing edges at right angles with a planer. It's designed to allow you to easily line up your target. The board includes stepped construction so that the planer can be used horizontally.

2 The fence is fixed at right angles to the 'corridor' (the area where your piece sits) so that the edge of the wood can be made into a right-angle cut.

3 Using a plate-shaped movable fence allows you to easily shave the wood down to the target width.

4 The width of the finished piece can be set in advance by accurately positioning the fence width with a ruler and/or calipers, as shown. Also, if the fence is set at an angle, the piece can be tapered.

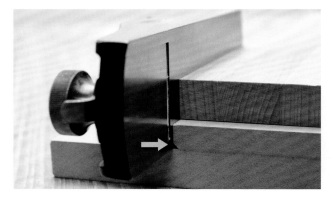

5 People often think that the planer board, meaning the piece that the planer butts up against, will end up being cut into. However, this is not the case. After your first pass, only the shoulder gap of the planer (the part without a blade, marked with an arrow) will touch it, so there won't be any damage after that first pass.

6 If you flip the shooting board over, it can be used as a bench hook because the cleat part becomes a fence.

MITRE PLANING TABLE

Mitre joints are used a great deal in the production of boxes. To make mitre joints, ends are most often cut at a 45-degree angle, which hides the cut and creates a beautiful finished product. The entire end must be cut to exactly 45 degrees, so high levels of precision are required. I will show you how I made the wood portion of this jig myself in conjunction with planer board metal brackets (the black metal part in the photo).

Mitre joint box

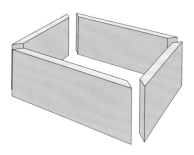

This convenient cutting table can perform three functions with just the one unit: it can cut 45-degree angles, shave a piece to the proper width and make right-angle cuts. The accuracy of the table may vary slightly from the 45-degree target, depending on who makes it. Don't worry if there is a small gap when the box is dry fit though – it can be corrected by tilting the planer blade a little bit.

Components

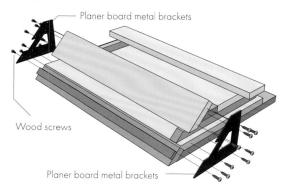

Planer board metal brackets

Wood screws

Planer board metal brackets

The custom wood parts are sandwiched between the triangular planer board metal brackets. Use 15mm thick MDF.

Cutting dimensions

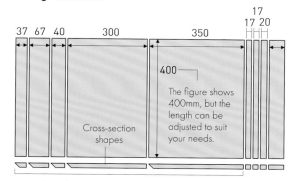

37 67 40 300 350 17 17 20

400

The figure shows 400mm, but the length can be adjusted to suit your needs.

Cross-section shapes

These five pieces will have 45-degree edges. **Unit: mm**

Installation diagram

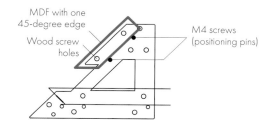

MDF with one 45-degree edge

Wood screw holes

M4 screws (positioning pins)

This is the method for securing the processed materials in the exact position. When attaching the MDF board with one 45-degree cut edge (red outline), insert the required M4 screws into the planer board metal brackets and then use them as positioning pins. Adjust the MDF board carefully in the bracket and then fix solidly with wood screws. (See Suppliers on page 275).

RIGHT-ANGLE AND WIDTH PLANER

Planing right-angled ends

The wood is slid in from the side and pressed up against the fence. Then, it can be cut to a proper right angle.

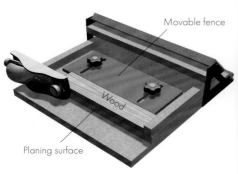

Planing long edges

Attaching a movable fence and thus fixing the distance from the cutting surface allows you to cut your material to the desired width every time.

MAKING A BOX WITH OUR MITRE PLANING TABLE

1 It would take a really long time to cut edges all the way to 45 degrees with a planer, so it's best to make a guide for rough cutting and first saw the pieces to approximately 45 degrees to speed things up.

2 If you are using thin pieces of wood, you can plane them to exactly the same length by first joining them with masking tape, etc., and processing them as a single piece. This way the same length of cut can be removed on each stroke. If the angle needs to be fine-tuned, it's best to just change the planer blade angle, rather than trying to shift the taped pieces.

3 Alternatively, the same effect can be achieved by applying double-sided tape to either side of the planer bottom. This will shift the planer angle itself a tiny bit. DO NOT remove the film on the outside of the double-sided tape! This will allow the planer to slide nicely in the jig while still changing the angle of the cut by the set amount.

MITRE JIG

Mitre cutting guide (see page 172).

Attach both 45-degree pins to the aluminium cross-cut guide and process to create mitres (see page 63).

Mitre joints are typically used in picture frames. You can either make your own mitre guide or use the aluminium cross-cut guide mitre function we used previously. In this section, we will show you how to use a mitre jig to correct small gaps in your 45-degree cuts on both rails and stiles. After that, we'll show you how to make a picture frame with a mitre jig and how to make the jig itself.

We'll make the type of jig shown in the figure on the opposite page and in photos **1** and **2** on the left. Photo **3** shows a technique that involves placing a piece of folded paper shim between the jig and wood. This shim allows us to change and correct tiny variances in angle. In this case, there was a gap inside the mitre joint, so we need to cut the 'outer' tip. Photo **4** shows that there was a gap on the outside of the mitre joint. So, in opposition to what we just did in photo **3**, we need to change the paper shim position and shave off the 'inside' edge of the tip.

How to use the mitre jig

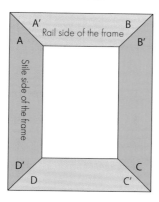

When making a picture frame like the one above, mark your pieces **A** through **D'**. Use your right hand to make the 45-degree cuts on **A**, **B**, **C** and **D**. For the ends with the dashes ['] – meaning all the ends from **A'** to **D'** – turn the mitre jig around and cut with your left hand.

To make sure that lengths are the same, it's best to line up the tips you are testing, and then touch them with your fingertips. Once you are certain that one set of tips isn't misaligned and everything feels flush, you can check the others. At this point, if you feel even the slightest bump, adjust the length by shaving off the excess. The stepped mitre jig fence thickness, shown below, is about 1 to 3mm thicker than the distance between the shoulder gap, meaning the area on the sole of the planer where there is no blade (see step 5 on page 164).

Dimensional drawing for mitre jig

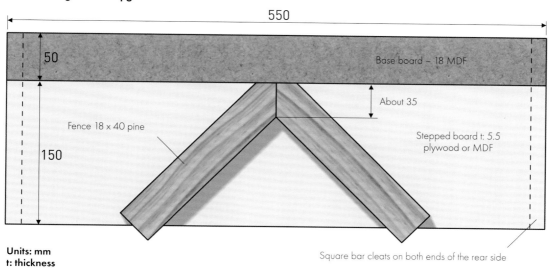

Units: mm
t: thickness

HOW TO MAKE A MITRE JIG

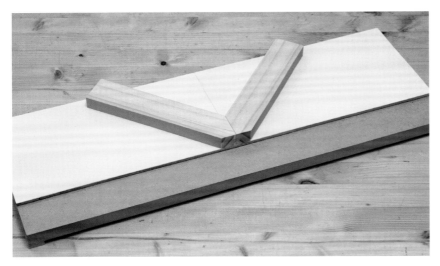

1 This is a planing table with two right-angle fences projecting out at 45 degrees. There are hooks at both ends on the back side so it can be hooked onto the workbench for both left-handed and right-handed cutting.

2 Fasten one right-angle fence to the stepped board. Use a speed square and instant glue to attach the fence at precisely 45 degrees. After roughly trimming off the overhanging tip of the fence, turn your planer on its side and run it along the edge of the stepped board to make sure everything is flush.

3 Use a carpenter's square, or similar tool, to line up the other fence. Then, glue it in place. Finish this protruding tip with a planer as well.

4 Apply glue to the entire back side of the step board and glue it to the base board.

5 Apply force evenly – with as many clamps as possible – and secure the step board to the base board.

6 Carefully apply sandpaper to both sides of the fence to prevent your pieces from slipping.

7 Glue both cleats on the back to complete the project.

MITRE CUTTING GUIDE WITH T-SHAPED STOPPER

MITRE CUTTING GUIDE CHART

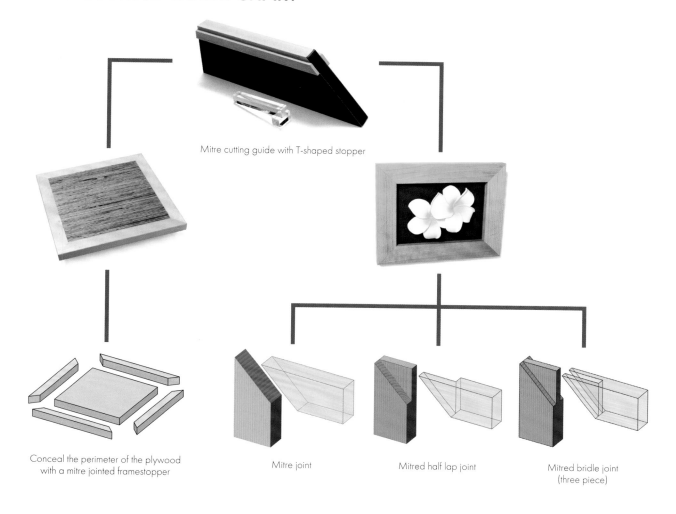

Mitre cutting guide with T-shaped stopper

Conceal the perimeter of the plywood with a mitre jointed framestopper

Mitre joint

Mitred half lap joint

Mitred bridle joint (three piece)

With this guide, you can process not only regular mitre joints – like those used in photo frames – but also joints designated as 'mitred OO joints'. If you use the guide together with a square acrylic T-shaped stopper, you can also make precise 45-degree corner cuts.

For mitre joints, each of the rails and stiles must be cut at exactly 45 degrees and must be the same length. If not, there will be gaps in the finished product.

This mitre guide accurately cuts material to 45 degrees, and the T-shaped stopper serves to maintain the exact length. Even if the frame front is decorated, and therefore uneven, the mitre joint can still be completed accurately if the back side is flat.

A mitre jointed frame hides the plywood perimeter cross-section of the MDF and the guide is useful for helping to glue the framing material to the plywood or MDF edge.

The guide is easy to make and performs extremely well. Fixing the two fences with double-sided tape at first means you can reattach them if the 45-degree angle isn't accurate enough during test cutting and after you have assembled everything.

MITRE CUTTING GUIDE DIMENSIONS

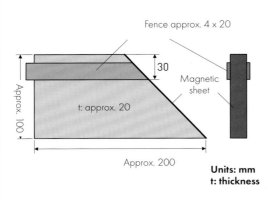

Fence approx. 4 x 20

Magnetic sheet

30

Approx. 100

t: approx. 20

Approx. 200

Units: mm
t: thickness

CUTTING ACCURATE MITRES

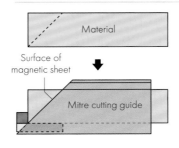

Material

Surface of magnetic sheet

Mitre cutting guide

T-shaped stopper
(10 x 10 acrylic square bar)

Place the T-shaped stopper on the corner of the material and align the magnetic sheet surface of the mitre guide with the stopper to accurately determine the cutting position (see steps 2 and 3 on page 182).

MITRE CUTTING GUIDE PRODUCTION SEQUENCE

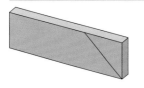

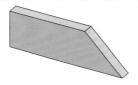

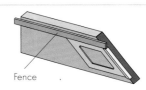

Fence

1 Mark one side of the wood at about 45 degrees.

2 Use a cross-cut guide, or the like, and cut at 45 degrees. It doesn't have to be exact (see step 1 opposite).

3 Attach the magnetic sheet (see step 2 opposite).

4 Place the tongue of the speed square on the magnetic sheet and then attach the fence with double-sided tape (see step 8 on page 176).

5 Cut off the end of the fence (see step 12 on page 177).

6 Attach the fence to the other side in the same manner (see step 13 on page 177).

7 Cut off the fence end to finish (see step 13 on page 177).

8 Apply sandpaper to both sides if necessary for your projects.

T-SHAPED STOPPER PRODUCTION SEQUENCE

 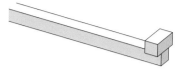 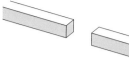

1 Cut off a 20mm piece of 10 x 10 acrylic square bar (see step 14 on page 177).

2 Glue the cut piece at a right angle. The end should project about 5mm from each end (see step 15 on page 177).

3 Cut to about 70mm and you're done (see step 16 on page 177).

HOW TO MAKE A MITRE CUTTING GUIDE WITH A T-SHAPED STOPPER

1 The main body of the guide is made of laminated wood. It has already been cut at about 45 degrees here. The other materials are: fence material, magnetic sheeting (with an adhesive side) and the acrylic square bar (see step 2 opposite).

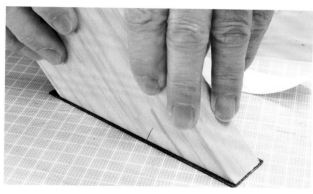

2 Attach the magnetic sheet to the 45-degree side of the guide (see step 3 opposite).

3 Cut off the protruding parts with a box cutter.

4 Press the magnetic strip down firmly, especially around the perimeter, with a roller if you have one.

5 Mark a spot 30mm from the top edge. This is the location of the bottom edge of the fence.

6 Attach the double-sided tape to the fence material. Make sure to apply it all the way across the piece so that it can be firmly fixed.

7 Apply double-sided tape to the speed square, slightly down from the tongue.

8 Place the speed square on the guide and hold it firmly against the 45-degree surface. Remember to attach the square at the 30mm mark. The precision of this determines the accuracy of the guide, so work carefully (see step 4 on page 174).

9 Apply the fence material to the guide body while holding it against the top of the speed square. This operation is also very important. Make sure that the fence material does not move, even slightly.

10 Once the fence is attached, carefully peel off the speed square.

11 Remove double-sided tape from the back of the triangular section of the protruding fence.

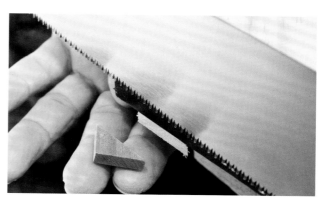

12 Cut off the triangular overhang with a saw. Leave the rear overhang intact. If there is any problem with the fence angle, you can reattach it after a test cut. This completes the fence installation on one side (see step 5 on page 174).

13 Attach the fence to the other side of the guide in the same way (see steps 6 and 7 on page 174).

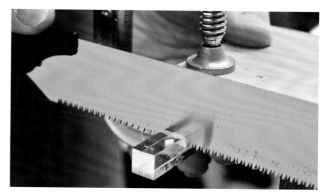

14 Cut a 10 × 10 square acrylic bar at 20mm. Fix the bar to the cross-cut guide and cut it with a pipe saw flat 225 for a clean cross-section. The 'flat' means it will have a straight-toothed replacement blade (see step 1 on page 175).

15 Glue the 20mm acrylic square bar to the remaining piece of acrylic bar. Use a square to maintain right angles and glue so that there is a 5mm overhang at each end. Be sure to use acrylic glue (see step 2 on page 175).

16 After the glue has set, cut the bar at about 70mm (see step 3 on page 175).

USING THE 45-DEGREE ANGLE ON A COMBINATION SQUARE

1 Apply double-sided tape to the ruler part.

2 Attach the square with the 45-degree side facing the magnetic sheet. Cut the fence material at 45 degrees beforehand, then place it against the steel square. Fix with instant glue or double-sided tape.

EVOLUTION OF THE MITRE CUTTING GUIDE

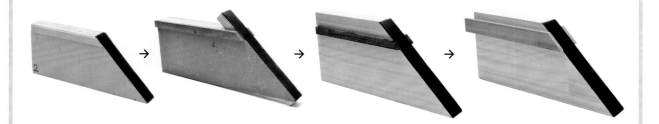

The first picture on the left is the initial guide. The second has a square bar glued on as shown. The magnetic strip is attached with double-sided tape because the angle-cut MDF surface was too rough for the strip to be attached directly. The result of this modification is that the saw blade contact area increases, and straight cuts become more stable. The next guide led to the final product on the far right, which includes the same advantages, but is easier to make. It also allows the fence to be reattached. The 45-degree guide has been in use for a long time, but if it is placed on the wood as is, the cut will depend on visual measurements and there will be deviations. That's when we came up with the idea of a T-shaped stopper. This eliminated visual measurement and dramatically increased accuracy.

The principles noted above have been commercialized and this product is machined with high precision from 20mm thick aluminium. It comes only with the aluminium body – no fence or magnetic sheet. Also, you will need to make the T-shaped stopper. However, the machining accuracy is excellent.

HOW TO USE THE T-SHAPED STOPPER

1 To avoid mistakes, use a pencil to draw diagonal lines in the direction of the mitres. Also, write all necessary information on the material, such as number, top, bottom, left, right, etc. Use a cross-cut guide and a length hook to cut precisely to dimension.

2 Place the T-shaped stopper on the outer corner as shown in the photo.

3 Align the mitre cutting guide fence with the wood. Place the magnetic sheet against the corner of the T-shaped stopper. This is the cut-off position. Clamp the material and mitre cutting guide to the workbench, taking care not to shift them.

4 Carefully cut the mitre section off. Be sure to cut in a straight line, as the way you cut determines accuracy.

5 Turn the mitre cutting guide over and cut the other end in the same way.

6 The photo shows a handscrew clamp. They are very convenient and can easily clamp the material and mitre cutting guide securely together.

7 After cutting off all eight mitres you can temporarily assemble the frame with rubber bands. If there are no gaps, just go ahead and glue the pieces together.

8 This is the back side. You can see the rabbet for accommodating the front glass plate and the backing board. Use the rabbeting guide for this process (see page 186).

ANGLE CORRECTION

Joining mitres together is a difficult process. Learn how to correct problems with a planer.

1 Correct any joint gaps during this temporary assembly stage. Determine whether the gap is on the heel or toe of the mitre and mark a line with a pencil so that the area that needs to be 'shaved down' is visible.

2 Correct problems with a planer, temporarily assemble, check the mitres and glue.

Decorative edging to hide end grain

You can outline the plywood or MDF edges with a mitre cut frame to produce a luxurious appearance. I will show you how to do this using the mitre cutting guide and mitre joints. Instead of a T-shaped stopper, we use a stop block cut out of scrap wood here.

DECORATIVE EDGE PRODUCTION SEQUENCE

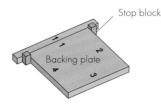

Stop block

Backing plate

1 Apply stop blocks at both ends of the backing plate (see step 3 opposite).

Mitre cutting guide

2 Butt the mitre cutting guide up to the stop block (see step 6 opposite).

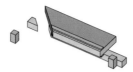

3 Remove the stop block and cut the mitre (see step 7 on page 184).

4 Turn the mitre cutting guide over and place against the remaining stop block (see step 8 on page 184).

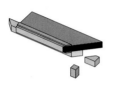

5 Remove the stop block and cut the mitre (see step 9 on page 184).

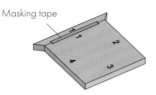

Masking tape

6 Glue the mitred piece to the backing plate or temporarily fix with masking tape (see step 10 on page 184).

7 Mitre the end of piece 2. If there are gaps in the joint, correct them with a planer (see step 11 on page 184).

8 Attach the stop block to the raw end of piece 2 (see step 12 on page 184).

9 Set the mitre cutting guide, remove the stop block and make your cut. Here, the mitre cutting guide is omitted (see step 12 on page 184).

10 Glue piece 2 to the backing board or fix it with masking tape to prevent it from shifting (see step 13 on page 184).

11 Mitre the end of piece 3. If there are any gaps with piece 2, correct them with a planer (see step 14 on page 184).

12 Attach the stop block to piece 3 (see step 14 on page 184).

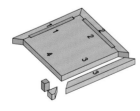

13 Set mitre cutting guide, remove stop block and cut the mitre. Do not glue or temporarily fasten piece 3 (see step 15 on page 185).

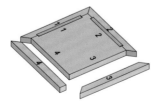

14 Mitre the end of piece 4. Correct any gaps in the joint with piece 1 (see step 16 on page 185).

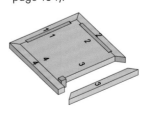

15 Attach stop block to piece 4 (see step 16 on page 185).

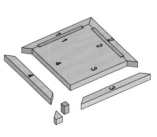

16 Set the mitre cutting guide, remove the stop block and cut the mitre. Glue everything together (see step 16 on page 185).

HOW TO MAKE A MITRE JOINTED FRAME

1 These are the laminated pieces that will become the backing plate and frame. Cut pieces a little bit long. Number all pieces and mark direction of mitre cuts.

2 Make sure the backing plate right angles are correct. Fix if necessary. If they are not at right angles, there will be gaps in the subsequent mitre joints.

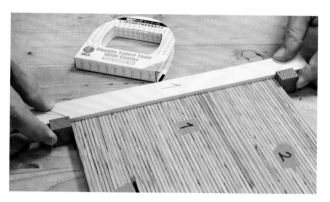

3 Place piece 1 against the backing plate 1. Add stop blocks that are about 10 × 20 to sandwich the backing plate and then attach with double-sided tape. The stop blocks should protrude about 5mm above the backing plate (see step 1 opposite).

4 Use stop blocks that aren't bevelled and have solid corners. Otherwise, their positioning will be slightly off.

5 Align the mitre cutting guide so that the magnetic sheet surface touches the stop block.

6 Clamp the material and the mitre cutting guide together. A handscrew clamp is used here (see step 2 opposite).

7 Remove the stop block and cut the mitre (see step 3 on page 182).

8 Turn the mitre cutting guide over and clamp the other stop block in place (see step 4 on page 182).

9 Remove the stop block and cut the mitre. This completes the mitre for piece 1 (see step 5 on page 182).

10 Glue, or use double-sided tape and masking tape, to temporarily fix piece 1 to the backing plate to prevent it from shifting. Use a speed square for accuracy. The square can also be temporarily fixed in place with tape (see step 6 on page 182).

11 Next, we need to trim the end of piece 2. Cut the end butting up to piece 1 (see step 7 on page 182).

12 Attach a stop block to the backing board and cut the mitre with the aid of the stop block (see steps 8 and 9 on page 182).

13 After cutting the mitre, temporarily fasten piece 2 to the backing plate with double-sided tape and/or masking tape to prevent it from shifting (see step 10 on page 182).

14 In the same manner, cut one end of piece 3 and attach the stop block on the other side of the backing plate. If there is a gap in the joint, correct it with a planer (see steps 11 and 12 on page 182).

15 Both ends of piece 3 are now mitred. This piece will not be glued or temporarily fastened to the backing plate at this stage (see step 13 on page 182).

16 Mitre one end of piece 4, attaching a stop block to the other end. Cut the mitre (see steps 14, 15 and 16 on page 182).

17 Align pieces 4 and 3, check for gaps in the joints and correct if necessary. After that, it is time to glue.

18 Apply glue and secure by four-way clamping. Clamp horizontally as normal, then use C-clamps to secure the joint tops. This will prevent vertical displacement. Once the glue has hardened, everything can be planed flat.

RABBETING GUIDE

This guide is for rabbeting wood. It's very useful for cutting the 'steps' inside the opening of a photo frame, or for lid inlaying inside the body of a box. First, please refer to the 'Rabbeting guide schematic diagram' opposite to grasp the construction steps. Then, we will show you in detail how to rabbet edges for a picture frame.

Rabbeting guide dimensions

The size of the guide and the thickness of the material are up to you.

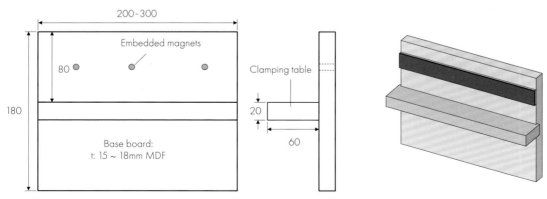

200-300

Embedded magnets

80

180

Base board:
t: 15 ~ 18mm MDF

Clamping table

20

60

Units: mm/ t: thickness

RABBETING GUIDE PRODUCTION SEQUENCE

Base board:
t: 15 ~ 18mm
MDF

Clamping table

1 Prepare the base board and clamping table material. These may be cut from the same MDF.

Chiselled slot

2 Chisel out a slot in the main body (this can be made without a slot).

3 Glue the table piece to the base. If there is no slot, reinforce with wood screws from the other side.

Spacer

4 Make a plywood spacer (about 20mm wide) with a magnetic sheet attached. Use double-sided tape to attach it at a position that matches the size of the material to be processed.

SCHEMATIC DIAGRAM OF RABBETING GUIDE IN USE

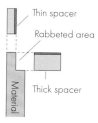

Thin spacer

Rabbeted area

Material

Thick spacer

1 The amount of rabbeting is determined by the thickness of the spacer.

Rabbeting guide

Clamping table

Base

Material

2 Attach a thin spacer to the flat face of the rabbeting guide with double-sided tape. Fix the guide to the material with clamps (see 'A' on page 188, and step 3 on page 189).

Material

3 Cut with a depth stop affixed to your blade. It is best to use a thick spacer for the stop (see steps 5 and 7 on page 190).

Material

4 Remove the thin spacer and the material.

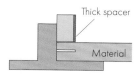

Thick spacer

Material

5 Clamp the rabbeting guide and the material together. Apply thick spacers to the clamping table section of the guide (see 'B' on page 188 and step 8 on page 191).

Material

6 Cut the rabbet. A depth stop can be attached to the saw blade (see step 12 on page 191).

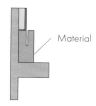

Material

7 For very narrow material, such as a photo frame, you can use the clamping table as a brace. The cut depth must be measured to that of the thick spacer. Use a depth stop (see step 14 on page 192 and 'C' on page 188).

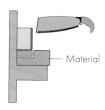

Material

8 Use thicker spacers. Clamp material horizontally and cut the rabbet to complete the process (see 'D' on page 188 and step 15 on page 192).

EXAMPLES OF RABBETING GUIDE USE

A

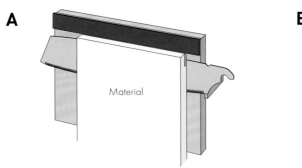

B

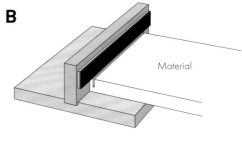

If you change the rabbeting guide direction, you can rabbet wide pieces as shown in figures A and B. Sometimes, as in figure A, the saw blade spacer is inserted by following the rule: **'If you can see the area marked with an O, insert a saw blade spacer'.** If the material is too wide, shift the rabbet guide, re-fasten and repeat the cutting process.

C

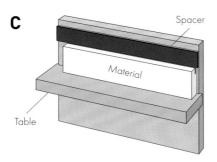

D

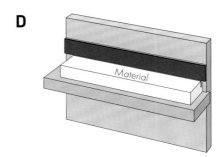

If the material is narrow, as shown in figure C, you can place it on the clamping table and attach a spacer above the piece. If the material is too long, shift the rabbeting guide, re-fasten and repeat the cutting process.

RABBETING A LONG PIECE OF WOOD

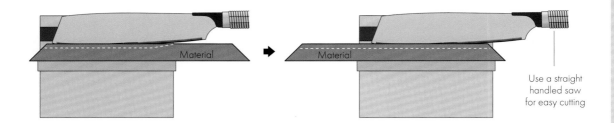

If the wood is too long, it can be shifted in the middle of the cutting operation as shown in the figure.

HOW TO MAKE A RABBETING GUIDE

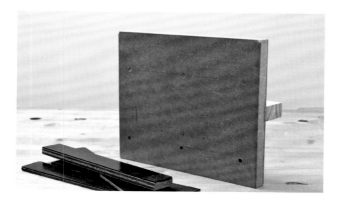

1 This is the first rabbeting guide I made. The base has magnets embedded in it and spacers can be attached as needed. These are used according to the maxim: **'If you can see the area marked with an O, insert a saw blade spacer'**. In the foreground, you can see spacers of different thicknesses. The guide is quite easy to make, so go ahead and make one and get accustomed to using it (see page 187).

2 This is the second guide I made. The clamping table is a bit wider, and its position can be changed according to wood size.

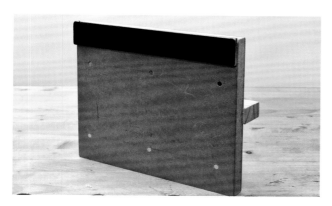

3 Spacers are attached with double-sided tape as shown in step 2 of the schematic diagram on page 187, and figure A opposite. The next step is to set the cut depth.

4 Set the cut depth by placing the saw blade on the setting guide (see page 30). Use the thickness of the spacer to attach a depth stop to the saw blade with double-sided tape. Setting is complete. The cut depth will be 10.3mm as written on the spacer.

5 Clamp the rabbeting guide to the board (see step 3 of the schematic diagram on page 187).

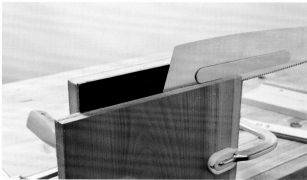

6 Cut into the end of the wood to the depth stop.

7 The material is wider than the rabbeting guide, so we need to shift the material and re-clamp it. Cut to the desired depth all the way across (see step 3 of the schematic diagram on page 187).

8 To finish the rabbet, reset the guide and the wood in a horizontal position. The piece on the right is scrap the same thickness as the guide to use as a sleeper for holding the wood level. The guide is clamped to the workbench (see step 5 on page 187).

9 Place the wood on the rabbeting guide. You can see that the sleeper is keeping the wood level.

10 Fix a spacer to the clamp table with double-sided tape. The material is actually quite wide, so we recommend floating the spacer 1 to 2mm above the material. This will make it easier to shift over and re-cut.

11 After securing material with a clamp, start cutting. Shift the material and continue cutting as necessary.

12 The rabbet has now been cut off (see step 6 of the schematic diagram on page 187).

13 The rabbeting process is now complete. Here, the spacer is sticking up over the top of the clamp table. That is because the table is quite low. We recommend making the clamp table about 60mm, as shown on page 186, 'Rabbeting guide dimensions'.

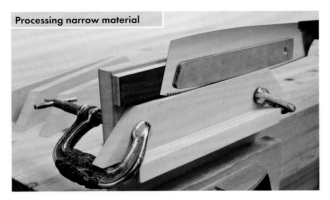

14 The photo shows the rabbeted photo frame material. Given that the material is quite thin (40mm), we decided to cut it on the clamping table portion of the rabbeting guide (see step 7 on page 187).

15 You can now lay the piece on its side and cut out the rabbet. The spacer will be too far up so lower it down close to the material and fix it in place (see step 8 on page 187).

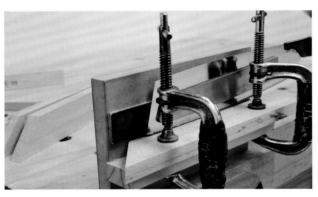

16 Make the cut. The saw blade in the photo has a brass depth stop. It is attached with double-sided tape. Making the saw blade heavier in this way allows for easier cutting.

17 The unwanted portion has been cut out.

18 In the rabbeting process, the maxim: **'If you can see the area marked with an O, insert a saw blade spacer'**, may be applied. For example, when processing the lid and body of a box.

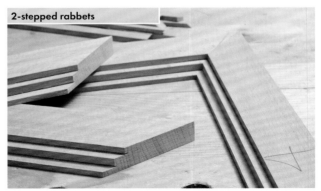

2-stepped rabbets

19 Stair-like rabbets can be placed inside the photo frame for decoration. Cut these with different thicknesses of spacers and depths of cut.

SELF-ALIGNING GROOVE CUTTING GUIDE/ACCURATE GUIDE

These guides are used specifically for grooving. The distance between the two serrations (cuts) that will become the groove can be self-set. This function sets the groove width equal to the material thickness by placing cut-offs in the groove cutting guide. It was originally developed and commercialized after obtaining a patent. The original was attached to a router for grooving tailstock joints and dovetail tailstock joints. I have applied the principles from that patent to the unique methods used in this book (reproduction is prohibited). As shown in the chart on page 194, the Accurate Guide is systemized and can be used in two main ways: by itself or in combination with accessories.

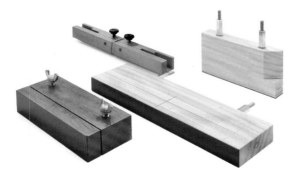

Left: the first Accurate Guide created for the unique methods used in this book. Centre: a model that uses the same principle, but is easier to make. Right: bottom of Accurate Guide. The diagonally cut area is a space for holding with your finger. Back: US-made self-aligning groove cutting guide for a router.

Accurate Guide

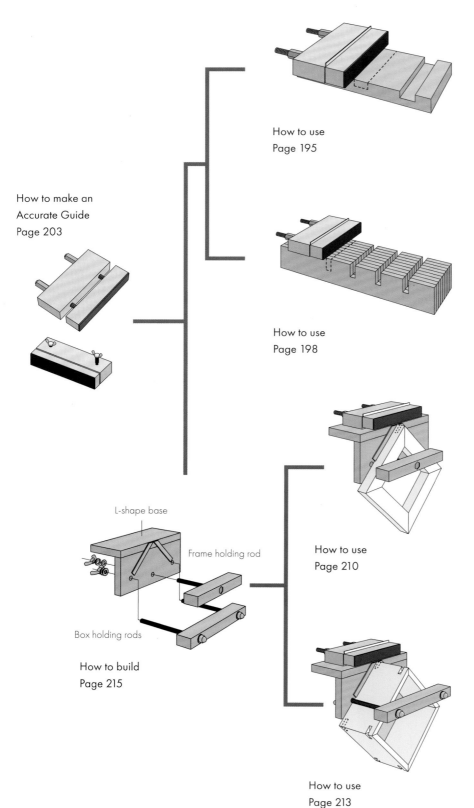

How to make an
Accurate Guide
Page 203

How to use
Page 195

How to use
Page 198

L-shape base

Frame holding rod

Box holding rods

How to build
Page 215

How to use
Page 210

How to use
Page 213

HOUSING JOINT
If you use a chisel or router plane to remove material from between the two cuts made by your guide, you will be able to make the very precise housing joints needed for shelving.

HALF LAP JOINT LATTICE
Using the Accurate Guide to cut material that has been taped together greatly increases efficiency.

MITRE JOINT REINFORCEMENTS
Groove width for the mitre joints is equal to the thickness of the reinforcing spline inserts in this joint.

SPLINE REINFORCEMENTS FOR LARGE MITRE JOINTS
The groove width can be easily set equal to the thickness of the spline that reinforces these large mitre joints.

HOUSING JOINTS

For spacers, use blades that are the same thickness as the saw blade you are using, and use straight-toothed blades. The saw blade spacer seen in the foreground is a 0.4mm thick straight-toothed replacement blade. At the back is a 0.6mm thick straight-toothed replacement blade. Both have been cut with tin snips to fit the Accurate Guide. I use a Japanese flush-cut straight-toothed saw (0.6mm thick) here, but I made two types of spacers so that I could also use the 0.4mm thick blade for fine work. In the background, you can see a machined housing joint. We will show you how to make one in this section (see page 29 for details on the saw).

How to make housing joints

1 Insert a saw blade spacer, of the same thickness as the saw, into the guide

2 Align the magnetic sheet with a marked line on the target piece and fix the guide with a clamp. Then, make the first cut. For convenience you can attach a depth stop to the saw blade with double-sided tape so that you can cut to a certain depth. Now we have one side of the housing joint groove cut.

3 Remove the saw blade spacer and insert either the wood you will use for the housing joint itself or a cut-off of the same width. Be sure to push the cut-off all the way down.

4 Make the second cut. Once the left and right housing joint cuts are made, remove the Accurate Guide.

5 Roughly chisel out the groove. It will be easier to work if you make several extra cuts between the two joint cuts. These can be made freehand, just make sure the depths remain constant by using a depth stop.

6 Set the groove depth on the router plane and finish to that depth.

7 Here is the completed housing joint. If you need to make the joint looser, insert pieces of paper on each side of the cut-off in step 3. This will widen the groove a bit. If you want to make it tighter, sandwich a piece of paper between the saw blade spacer and the side of the guide in step 1. This will move the initial cut over a tiny bit and make the groove tighter. Be sure to make a test cut or two before moving on to the real thing.

ANOTHER WAY TO MAKE A HOUSING JOINT

1 For this method, we sandwich a cut-off (or our actual piece) between two blocks with magnetic sheets attached. Then we make the outside two cuts.

2 Use a saw with a depth stop attached to make the first and second cuts. Change your sawing direction so that the depth stop doesn't need to be moved.

3 Finish the groove to a consistent depth with a router plane.

4 Here is the completed joint.

IF THE FIT IS TOO TIGHT

You can shave the edge of the material to be inserted into the groove with a planer as needed.

MAKING A HALF LAP JOINT LATTICE

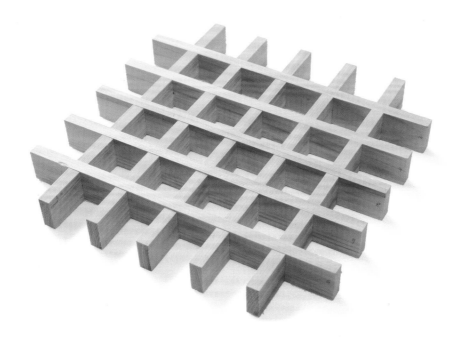

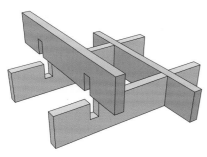

The structure of the latticework is based on the use of cross half lap joints, where the lattice pieces are cut halfway through and then laid one over the other. The work is done by taping together the required number of pieces and then cutting the half lap joints with an Accurate Guide. The dimensions of the material in the photo are 240 x 28 x 9mm.

How to make a half lap joint lattice

1 Cut out the necessary number of pieces of wood and secure them with masking tape on the front and back. This will prevent them from moving when they are being cut.

2 Mark the taped block in six equal sections. These lines will form the centreline of each cut.

3 Mark lines on the material 4.5mm to one side of the previous centre mark. These lines are where you will first align the Accurate Guide. The grooving at the other end is done by turning the material around and using the proper spacers.

4 Insert a saw blade spacer of the same thickness as the actual saw blade used in the guide. The saw is a Japanese flush-cut saw with a straight-toothed blade that is 0.6mm thick, so a spacer with a thickness of 0.6mm is used here.

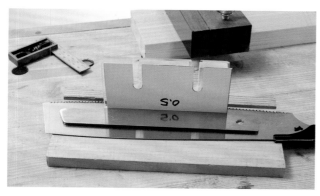

5 Attach a depth stop to the saw blade. The depth of the cut should be half the width of the wood.

6 Make sure the guide is at right angles, then clamp.

7 Make the first cut along the marked and squared position.

8 Remove the saw blade spacer and pinch two cut-offs of the proper size in the guide.

9 This is the second cut. The groove width is determined by the spacers.

10 Repeat the process above for each mark on the tape.

11 For the final grooves, there is not enough space to clamp down the guide, so the material is flipped around.

12 The material has been flipped around. Place the square on the same side as before and clamp down the guide.

13 After making the first cut using the saw blade spacer, go ahead and make the second cut with the two cut-offs as spacers.

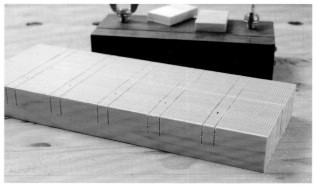

14 All cuts are now complete.

15 Remove the tape. Be sure to number each piece of material at this time.

16 Scribe exactly half the width of the material (even if that is slightly less than the bottom end of the cuts as seen here).

17 The back and front of each piece has now been scribed.

18 Use a chisel to notch out the grooves at each scribed line.

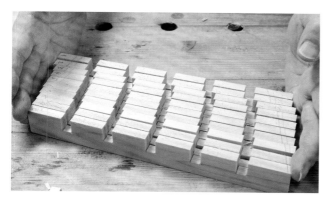

19 Processing is now complete.

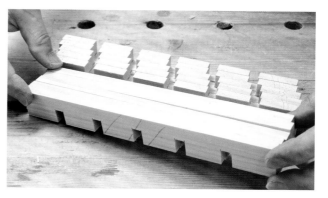

20 Turn over half of the pieces and prepare to assemble.

21 Carefully perform a temporary dry assembly to prevent breakage. Check that everything fits correctly.

22 Disassemble and sand the pieces all together. This should smooth the top surface nicely and remove any marks.

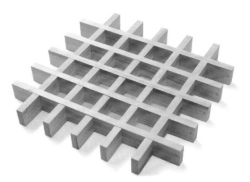

23 Reassemble to complete.

Putting vertical and horizontal pieces together

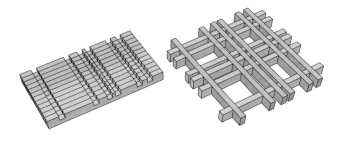

24 This lattice can be made without dividing the wood into equal parts. Feel free to try different patterns.

HOW TO MAKE AN ACCURATE GUIDE

Here is the latest version of the guide, which is actually quite easy to make. Ideally, the saw blade spacer you use should be the same size and material as the actual saw blade. However, if such blades are too thick for tin snips then paper or acrylic sheets of the correct thickness can be used. Be aware that if the thickness varies by even 0.1mm, it will show up in your resulting cuts. Also note that it is convenient to have different sizes of Accurate Guides for different applications. Here we are making a guide for pieces of wood around 25mm thick. We will use M6 screws and M6 washers, a set of high nuts and one countersunk screw.

ACCURATE GUIDE PRODUCTION SEQUENCE

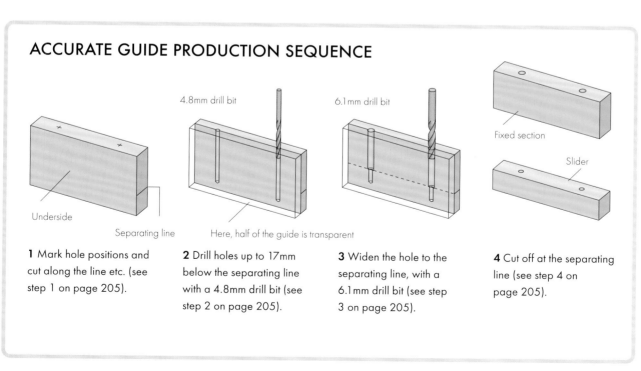

1 Mark hole positions and cut along the line etc. (see step 1 on page 205).

2 Drill holes up to 17mm below the separating line with a 4.8mm drill bit (see step 2 on page 205).

3 Widen the hole to the separating line, with a 6.1mm drill bit (see step 3 on page 205).

4 Cut off at the separating line (see step 4 on page 205).

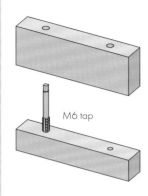

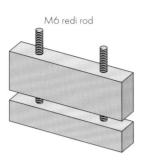

M6 redi rod

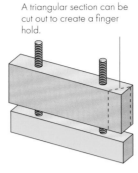

A triangular section can be cut out to create a finger hold.

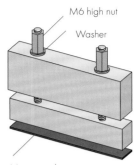

M6 high nut

Washer

Magnetic sheet

5 Use an M6 tap in the bottom hole of the slider to cut the threads (see step 7 on page 206).

6 Attach M6 all thread rods (ATR, or redi rod), about 110mm in length, to the slider (see step 11 on page 206).

7 Shave about 0.5mm off the bottom of the slider (yellow part) (see step 16 on page 207).

8 Attach a magnetic sheet to the slider. Do not use spring (split lock) washers (see step 20 on page 208).

Accurate Guide dimensions

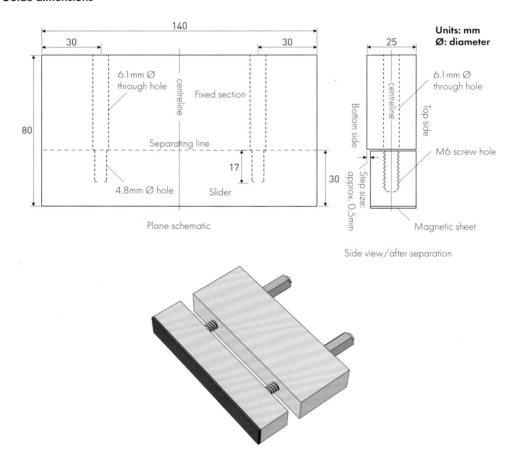

Units: mm
Ø: diameter

140

30

30

6.1mm Ø through hole

centreline

Fixed section

80

Separating line

17

4.8mm Ø hole

Slider

30

Plane schematic

25

centreline

Bottom side

Top side

6.1mm Ø through hole

M6 screw hole

Step size: approx. 0.5mm

Magnetic sheet

Side view/after separation

HOW TO MAKE AN ACCURATE GUIDE

Marking

1 Cut the wood and mark according to the schematic. In the photo, we used a 25mm thick piece of wood. However, a 20mm thick piece will work (see step 1 on page 203).

Drilling

2 Drill a 4.8mm hole. This is the diameter of the female threaded hole. The hole goes to 17mm below the separating line. As seen in the photo, a mortice jig was used to secure the material (see step 2 on page 203).

3 Replace with a 6.1mm drill bit and widen the hole, but only down to the separating line. The upper black line represents the separating line. The lower black line indicates the depth of the previously drilled 4.8mm hole (see step 3 on page 203).

Separating line

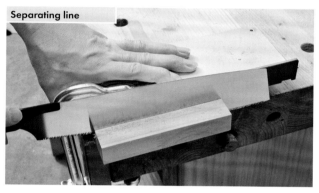

4 Cut along the separating line to divide the unit into the slider portion and fixed portion. As seen in the photo, an aluminium cross-cut guide is used here (see step 4 on page 203).

5 Once the pieces are separated, you can see that the hole diameters are different.

Tapping (threading)

6 The 4.8mm threads in the slider are made with a tap, several different types are shown here. Left to right, we see a taper tap, a plug tap and a bottoming tap. The bottoming tap is used here as there is a through hole and it has threads most of the way to the tip. This creates as many threads as possible in the slider.

7 Attach the bottoming tap to a drill chuck. Make sure the tap is perpendicular to the surface. Turn the chuck by hand to cut the threads and, for safety, unplug the power on the drill (see step 5 on page 204).

Cutting redi rod

8 Cut the M6 redi rod to the required length with a hacksaw. The two pieces should be about 110–120mm.

9 Hacksawed edges will always have burrs, which means the nut may not slide on nicely, so be sure to bevel the ends of the redi rod with a file.

Installing the screws

10 Once the high nuts are partially threaded onto the redi rod, insert a countersink screw until it butts up to the end of the rod. You can now use a screwdriver to crank the redi rod down.

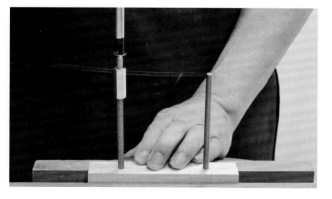

11 Screw the redi rod all the way into the slider (see step 6 on page 204).

Apply wax

12 Before assembling, be sure to apply wax (or similar) to the drilled holes and redi rod to make them slide easily.

13 Inspect the joints and correct any gaps.

14 To correct any tilt, you can hold the slider in a vice and push firmly on the fixed section.

Mark the top surface

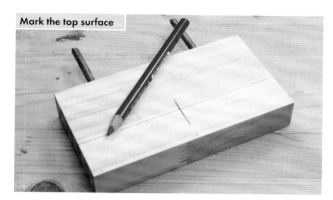

15 Mark the top of both the fixed section and the slider with red pencil so you can distinguish the top and bottom surfaces when disassembling and reassembling.

Planing underside of slider

16 We want to ensure fluid slider movement, even if the fixed section is clamped or taped down with double-sided tape, so we need to plane down the slider bottom by approximately 0.5mm (see step 7 on page 204).

Right-angle creation

17 Plane the fixed section bottom surface so that it is at right angles to the slider. At this point, the slider bottom is 'floating' a bit because we just planed it, so we need to plane with the bottom surface of the fixed part pressed firmly against the table as seen in the photo.

Saw blade spacer

18 It is best to use an actual saw blade as a spacer. However, saw blades are steel and can be very hard to cut, so a piece of paper or thin acrylic of the same thickness can be used instead.

Temporary assembly

19 Insert the saw blade, or other spacer, and assemble. Make sure everything fits perfectly before moving on.

Magnetic sheet

20 Attach the magnetic sheet to the slider. Also, install washers and high nuts (see step 8 on page 204).

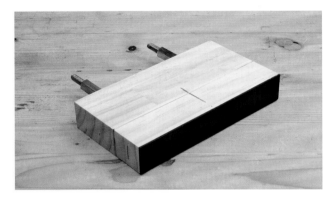

21 We use high nuts instead of wing nuts because the nuts don't need to be tightened very powerfully. The high nuts are actually easier to finger tighten. Always be careful not to overtighten during use.

PRINCIPLES AND USE OF THE ACCURATE GUIDE

EXAMPLE OF HOW TO SET GROOVE WIDTHS FOR HOUSING JOINTS

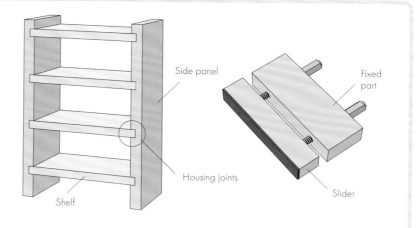

Side panel

Fixed part

Housing joints

Slider

Shelf

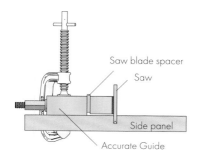

Saw blade spacer

Saw

Side panel

Accurate Guide

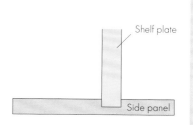

Shelf cut-off

Saw

Shelf plate

Side panel

1 With a saw blade spacer of the same thickness as your cutting blade inserted in the Accurate Guide, set the guide on the first marked-out line and cut.

2 Remove the saw blade spacer and place the shelf cut-off in the guide. Your second cut will now determine the width of the groove. Finally, carve out the groove.

3 The distance travelled by the slider is equal to the shelf thickness minus the saw blade thickness, so we don't add the saw blade thickness to the second cut. That way an accurate groove can be machined.

FINE ADJUSTMENT OF THE FIT

For housing joints try to make a test cut before moving on to the real thing. If the fit is too tight, widen the groove by inserting a piece of paper – together with the cut-off – into the Accurate Guide. If the fit is too loose, put a piece of paper between the saw blade spacer and the guide to narrow the groove width.

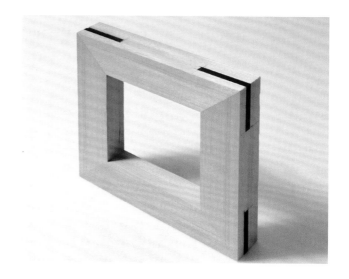

ACCESSORIES: HOW TO #1, REINFORCING FRAMES WITH SPLINES

1 Mitre joints generally lack durability because wood is glued directly to wood. To rectify this, we use spline reinforcements. Splines increase strength and enhance appearance. We only need our Accurate Guide and a few accessories.

2 Decide how deep to insert the splines and mark a 45-degree line with a speed square (arrow). Follow that line around to the side of the photo frame. This will mark the depth of the cut. Use a speed corner to mark each corner.

3 Cut splines that are larger than needed. These thin splines may not be uniform in thickness, so be sure to check them in several places with calipers.

4 Calculate where you want to cut into the photo frame and mark that on the bottom of the slider. Apply blue masking tape and draw lines with a magic marker. We'll call this the 'cutting line'.

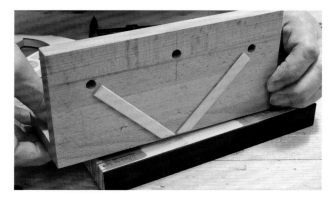

5 Align the edge of the L-shaped base (see page 216) with the cutting lines and fix with double-sided tape. Don't forget to insert a spacer of the same thickness as the saw used for the Accurate Guide.

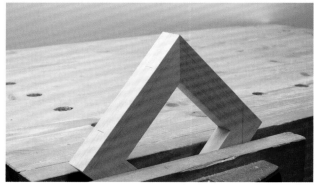

6 Fix the photo frame in a wood vice, as shown.

7 Hold the photo frame and the guide together with the frame holding rod.

8 This is how the frame and guide should look. You can see that the slider of the Accurate Guide is floating off the L-shaped base, and the corner of the photo frame is also lowered from the L-shaped base surface.

9 Make the first cut.

10 Once you have cut to the depth of the marked cut lines, attach a depth stop to the saw blade. This will give you a good reference for the cut depth.

11 Now that the first cut has been made, the spacer can be pulled out and spline pieces inserted. The second cutting position is now set.

12 Make the second cut.

13 You can see that parallel cuts have been made.

14 Cut out the spline slot, slightly above the cut line, with a coping saw. Finish with a chisel.

15 Use a thin chisel to carve to the centre of the mitre joint. After that, turn around and start carving from the other side until you reach the centre again.

16 If you make the bottom of the spline slot slightly V-shaped instead of completely flat, there will be no gaps at the edges of the splines. Place the chisel as shown and make sure that only the two outer sides of the chisel touch, not the centre.

17 When inserting a spline, it fits perfectly.

18 Apply glue to the spline slot and quickly insert the spline. If you go slowly, the material may swell, and things will become difficult.

19 Once the glue has hardened, cut off any protruding spline edges with a flat saw and finish with a planer.

ACCESSORIES: HOW TO #2, REINFORCING BOXES WITH SPLINES

Box reinforcement is the same as for photo frames. Here we use box holding rods in our jig. Look closely at how the lid and body are fixed in the diagram. The splining method is the same as for the photo frames noted above.

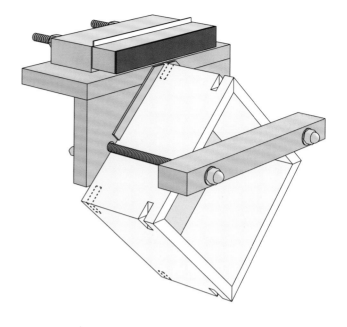

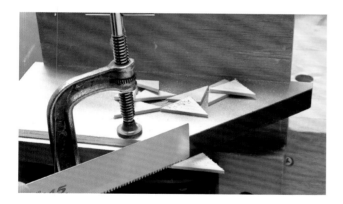

1 Cutting splines. The material is fixed in the guide and cut once, then the material is turned over and cut again. The guide used here is an aluminium cross-cut/mitre guide.

2 After first determining the position of your cuts, fix the box lid to the L-shaped base to complete the spline grooves.

3 After that the body of the box is clamped in the vice and cut.

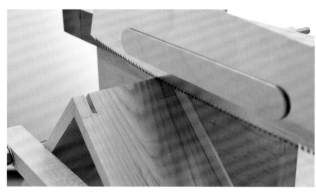

4 Cut the spline near the bottom of the box. When positioning, make sure that the floor of the box and the position of the spline do not overlap.

5 Glue in the splines.

6 Cut off the spline overhangs and finish with a planer to complete the project.

FABRICATION OF ACCURATE GUIDE ACCESSORIES

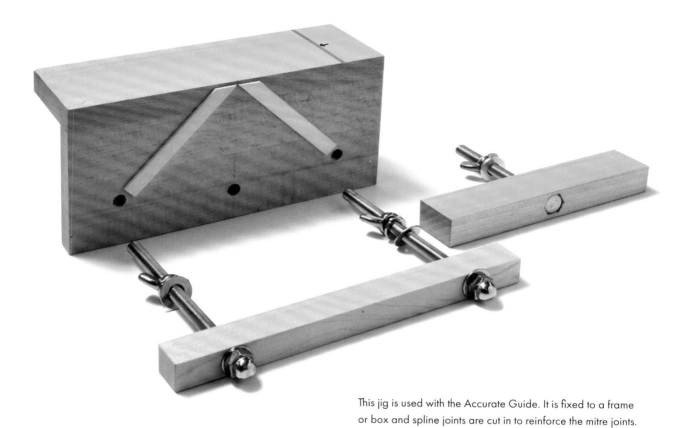

This jig is used with the Accurate Guide. It is fixed to a frame or box and spline joints are cut in to reinforce the mitre joints.

L-SHAPED BASE PRODUCTION SEQUENCE

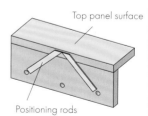

Top panel surface

Positioning rods

1 Prepare two pieces of wood 15mm thick, of the same length.

2 Glue them together at right angles, then sand any imperfections (see step 3 on page 217).

3 Drill three 8mm holes (see step 7 on page 218).

4 Use double-sided tape to affix the frame or box so that the corner is about 2mm below the top panel surface (see step 8 on page 218).

PICTURE FRAME HOLDING ROD PRODUCTION SEQUENCE

1 This piece can be any size as long as it spans the frame and holds firmly.

2 Drill a hole 6mm deep with a 13mm drill bit (see step 9 on page 218).

3 Drill an 8mm through hole (see step 10 on page 218).

4 Push the M8 hexagonal bolt through the hole and tap the hexagonal head into place (see step 11 on page 218).

BOX HOLDING ROD PRODUCTION SEQUENCE

1 The wood can be any size as long as it is wide enough and the box is held firmly.

2 Drill a preliminary hole with a 6.8mm drill bit (see step 12 on page 218).

3 Use an M8 tap to thread the hole (see step 13 on page 219).

Cap nut

4 Thread the M8 bolts through and lock with cap nuts (see step 15 on page 219).

DIMENSIONS

L-SHAPED BASE

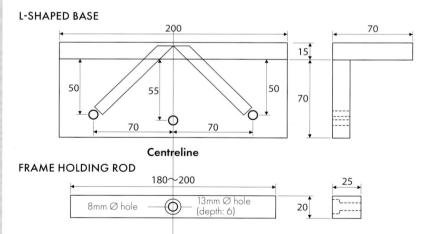

200

15

70

70

50   55   50

70   70

Centreline

FRAME HOLDING ROD

180～200

8mm Ø hole   13mm Ø hole
(depth: 6)

25

20

FRAME HOLDING ROD

200

70   70

M8 screw holes

25

20

Units: mm
Ø: diameter
t: thickness

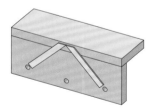

Aluminium angle material (50 x 75 x t5 unequal angle) can be substituted in this L-shaped base.

HOW TO MAKE AN ACCURATE GUIDE/ACCESSORY

1 Glue the base plates together in an L-shape. For accuracy, fix two pieces of scrap wood to the workbench with double-sided tape to serve as a temporary fence (see photo 3). The height of the fence should be greater than the thickness of the base board.

2 Tape the sides of the fence so that any glue overflow won't stick.

3 Glue the two base plates together while pressing them against the positioning fence. This is done while securing the right angle with two squares. Attach double-sided tape to the bottom of the squares to hold (see step 2 on page 215).

4 After gluing, the right angle of the L-shape can be adjusted.

5 Mark the position of the holes on the inside of the base and mark it with a punch.

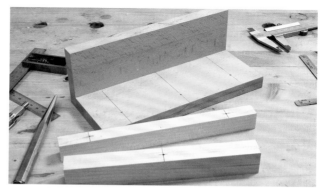

6 Using a punch or drill, mark the hole positions on the frame holding rod and the box holding rod. It is more efficient to do similar work all at once.

7 Drill an 8mm hole in the L-shaped base. If you use a sacrificial board under the base, the exit hole won't blow out. This will produce a nice clean hole (see step 3 on page 215).

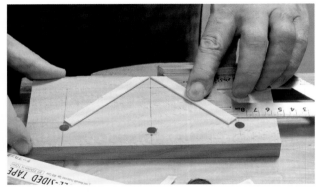

8 Attach positioning rods in a 45-degree-angled 'V' on the front centre of the L-shaped base using double-sided tape. Make sure that the frame, or box, to be fixed is positioned about 2mm lower than the top panel (see step 4 on page 215).

Two-stage hole for frame holding rod

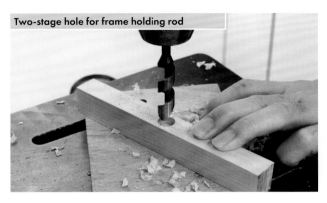

9 Make a hole 13 × 6mm deep, then gently tap in the head of an M8 hexagonal bolt (head diameter: approx. 14mm) (see step 2 on page 216).

10 Drill a through hole of 8mm. Now we have a two-stage hole of 13mm and 8mm (see step 3 on page 216).

11 Tapping in the M8 hexagonal bolt completes the installation (see step 4 on page 216).

Drilling holes for box holding rods

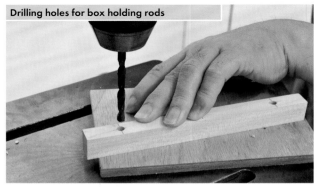

12 Drill two 6.8mm holes. These are the preparation holes for M8 bolts (see step 2 on page 216).

Machining threads with a tap

13 Attach M8 tap to the drill chuck and make sure the target material is perfectly horizontal. We will start threading by turning the chuck by hand, so be sure to unplug the machine (see step 3 on page 216).

14 Once the tap is running perfectly perpendicular to the material, you can continue to thread it using a tap handle.

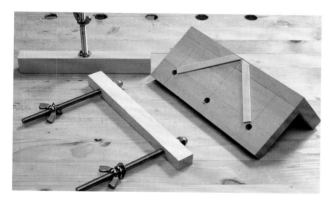

15 Thread the M8 bolts all the way through and lock with cap nuts to complete (see step 4 on page 216).

CASE MITRE CUTTING GUIDE

Boxes made with case mitre joints are beautiful because the end grain isn't visible. The difficulty with actually fabricating such boxes is that gaps may appear in the joints. If the 45-degree angle isn't correct, or the wood length isn't uniform, case mitre joints can't be made properly.

The two main characteristics to keep in mind with this guide are: 1) making sure the magnetic sheet surface is at an exact 45-degree angle, and 2) properly aligning and cutting the material to length.

First, the 45-degree angle of the magnetic sheet is set with two commercially available speed squares, then the angle is fixed with epoxy resin. Material length can be determined, and the cut adjusted, by widening the guide bridge to the left or right. The guides themselves will be around the same length as the material to be cut.

Fabrication requires: two speed squares, a flat piece of scrap wood, double-sided tape and two-component epoxy adhesive. See page 223 for guide instructions.

Make different sized guides and use them according to the size of your work.

CASE MITRE CUTTING GUIDE DIMENSIONS

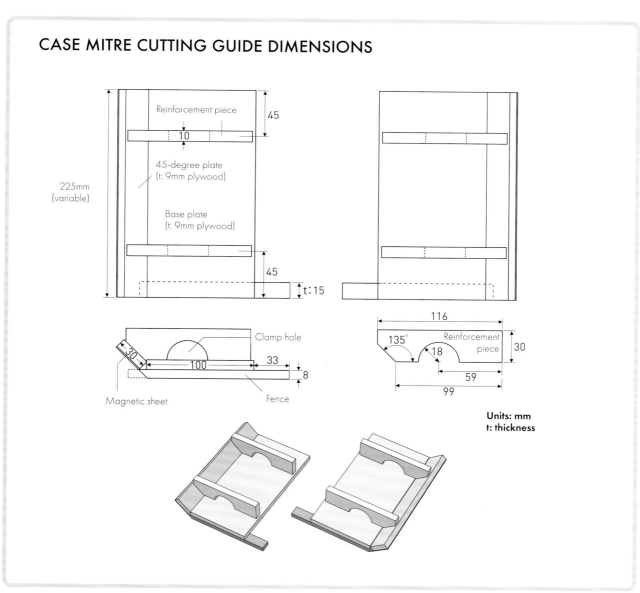

Reinforcement piece

45

10

45-degree plate
(t: 9mm plywood)

225mm
(variable)

Base plate
(t: 9mm plywood)

45

t: 15

Clamp hole

30

100

33

8

Magnetic sheet

Fence

116

135°

Reinforcement
piece

18

30

59

99

Units: mm
t: thickness

CASE MITRE CUTTING GUIDE PRODUCTION SEQUENCE

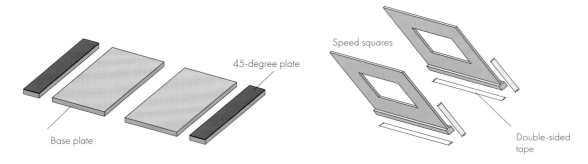

45-degree plate

Base plate

Speed squares

Double-sided tape

1 Cut the base and 45-degree plates. Attach the magnetic sheet to the 45-degree plate (see step 1 opposite).

2 Apply double-sided tape to the base and to the 45-degree sections of the speed squares (see step 12 on page 224).

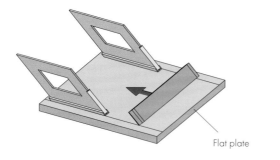

Flat plate

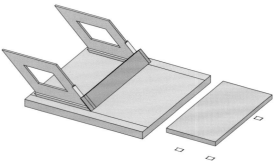

3 Stick the speed squares to a flat plate. Shift the 45-degree board over to the speed squares while keeping the bottom edge of the magnetic sheet in contact with the flat plate (see step 13 on page 225).

4 Affix small pieces of double-sided tape to the base plate in four locations, then attach the base to the flat plate while holding it against the 45-degree plate (see step 17 on page 225).

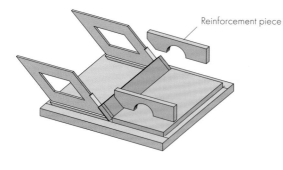

Reinforcement piece

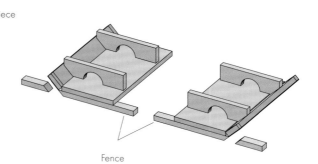

Fence

5 Put a generous amount of glue on the reinforcement pieces and glue them to the 45-degree plate and the base plate. Do not press down (see step 22 on page 226).

6 Attach the fence at a right angle and cut off any overhang with a saw (see step 30 on page 227).

HOW TO MAKE A CASE MITRE CUTTING GUIDE

1 Cut out two pieces of the 45-degree plate and two pieces of the base plate (see step 1 opposite).

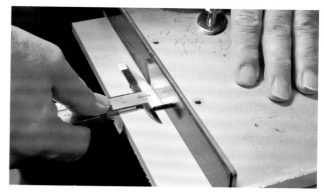

2 To cut out a 30mm wide 45-degree plate, use calipers to precisely determine the width.

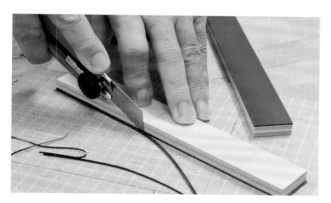

3 Attach a magnetic sheet to the 45-degree board.

Cutting out the reinforcement piece

4 Make semi-circular clamp holes by drilling holes in a piece of wood and then splitting it in half. Use a board that is slightly larger than needed and drill a 36mm diameter hole at 30mm from one end.

5 Two reinforcing plates add up to 60mm. Use calipers and a jig to cut them correctly. Attach a stopper as shown. The calipers and jig are also attached to the aluminium cross-cut guide.

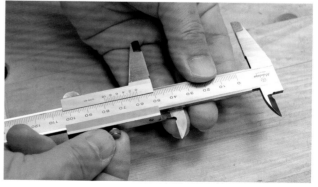

6 Here's the method for setting the calipers and ruler to the same length. First, set the caliper distance.

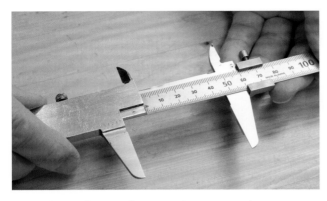

7 After you have set the proper distance using the upper jaws of the calipers, use the frame on the calipers to accurately set the distance on the ruler and tighten the stopper screw.

8 If you place the drilled wood as shown (long side facing out), it will be ready to cut to 60mm.

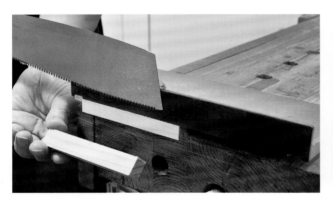

9 Clamp together the cross-cut guide and the wood underneath on the workbench. Now the wood can be properly cut to 60mm.

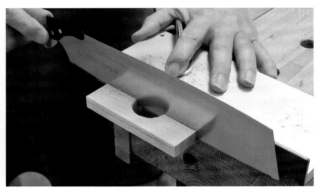

10 Divide the reinforcing plate in two. Position subsequent plates using calipers, a jig and a stopper as in step 5 on page 223.

11 The 45-degree cut on the reinforcement piece is made using a mitre guide (it doesn't have to be very precise).

12 Apply double-sided tape to each of the two speed squares, on the ruler base and the 45-degree part (see step 2 on page 222).

13 Attach the speed squares to the flat plate. The rulers should be parallel to each other and the edges should be aligned (see step 3 on page 222).

14 Peel off the double-sided tape's backing paper on the 45-degree sections.

15 At this point, it's easiest to move the magnetic sheet while keeping the bottom edge against the flat plate. Attach the magnetic sheet side of the 45-degree board to the speed squares.

16 The photo above shows where the 45-degree plate is glued to the speed square.

17 Attach short pieces of double-sided tape to the base plate in four places. Be careful, as if the tape is too long it will be difficult to remove later (see step 4 on page 222).

18 Move the base plate so that it touches the 45-degree plate, then lower the base plate and attach it to the flat plate.

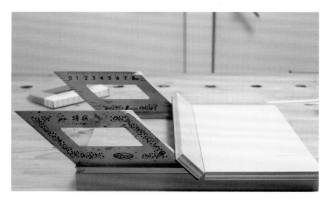

19 The base plate is now temporarily fixed.

20 Use a two-component epoxy for strength. First, mix the resin and hardener together.

21 Now spread a thin layer of epoxy on the reinforcement piece. Next, add a thin layer to the 45-degree plate and the base plate. Finally, add a generous layer to the reinforcement piece (to fill gaps).

22 Place the reinforcement piece, with a bulge of epoxy on it, in place. The trick is to just set it in place. Pressing down may cause the 45-degree angle to change. Gaps will be filled by the epoxy resin (see step 5 on page 222).

23 Do the same for the second reinforcement piece.

24 As you can see, there is quite a bit of epoxy sticking out. Don't worry, just let it cure.

25 Apply a generous amount of epoxy to the valleys where the 45-degree plate and base plate meet.

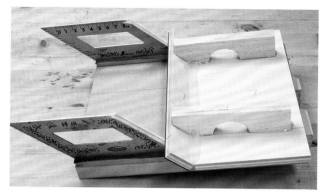

26 Tilt everything slightly so the glue stays in the valleys. Make another identical guide in the same manner as laid out above.

27 Leave overnight. Once the glue has cured, remove the guide from the double-sided tape.

28 To make an identical guide, do not remove the speed square from the flat plate. Rather, just replace the double-sided tape on the 45-degree section.

29 Finally, fill the valleys on the outside of the case mitre cutting guide with epoxy.

30 Install the fence. This must be set at right angles to the guide! Clamp the magnetic sheet edge to the flat plate as shown (see step 6 on page 222).

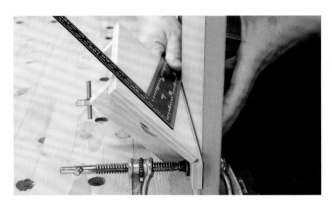

31 Flip upright and place the whole apparatus in a bench vice. Place the carpenter's square on top of the bench vice and place it against the base plate.

32 First, practise gluing the fence to the base plate while the square is still laying up against it. Lay the fence material down on the base plate along the square. Practise this two or three times. Instant glue is used for final fixing of the fence.

33 In the final stage, double-sided tape is attached to the square to prevent it from moving, then the glue is applied to the fence material and it is lowered onto the base.

34 As you can see, the fence material is glued in place with a slight protrusion on each side.

35 Glue the fence material to both guides.

36 Place your saw against the magnetic sheet surface of the guide and cut off the protruding fence material. The sawed-off surface is useful for positioning your target material (see step 6 on page 222).

37 The case mitre cutting guide is complete.

38 How to use: connect the two guides with a cut-off to set the length of the material to be cut off. Now you can cut multiple pieces of the same length. See page 101 for an example of actual use.

MORTICE AND TENON JOINT

A mortice and tenon joint is made using a hole and a corresponding projection. It is a very sturdy joint used frequently in furniture.

It is not that difficult to make a single mortice and tenon joint of course. But imagine a cabinet door. If there are four cross-braces and the frame material is made with mortice and tenon joints, there are four separate sets of mortices and four separate sets of tenons. If there are two doors, the total number of processed joint pieces will be sixteen, so an efficient, highly accurate and reliable method is needed.

The unique methods found in this book rarely use power tools. However, it does use a small drill press. The reason for this is that carving out holes while tapping a chisel with a mallet would actually make a lot of noise. Hand-held drills also make a lot of noise. However, small drill presses are very quiet.

Parts of a mortice and tenon joint

Figure 1

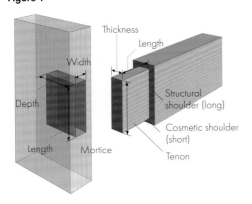

Thickness
Length
Width
Depth
Structural shoulder (long)
Cosmetic shoulder (short)
Length
Mortice
Tenon

Figure 2

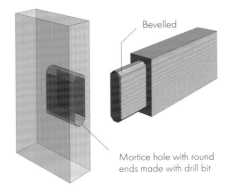

Bevelled

Mortice hole with round ends made with drill bit

HOW TO MAKE A MORTICE AND TENON JOINT

1 Drill a series of holes to create a long open space. This can then be made into a mortice. The holes should be located in the centre of the material. When drilling a continuous set of holes, you will notice that they are often slightly off-centre, even though the jig was centred! No problem. Just rotate the material 180 degrees, placing the opposite side against the jig, and drill again. With this method, holes can be accurately drilled every time.

DRILL BIT AND MORTICE HOLE SIZE

I have tried many different types of drill bits for mortices. The one that produced the best results was for bamboo.

2 The new-type vertical ripping guide is used to cut out the tenon. Tenons must be centred to correspond to the mortice. Inserting spacers ranging from 0.1 to 10mm into the guide body allows us to position the magnetic sheet properly and accurately determine the position for cutting into the target material in 0.1mm increments (see page 18). The saw blade has a self-made brass depth stop.

3 This mortice jig is designed to be fixed to the worktable of a drill press. Place your target material between the aluminium angle and the wooden lever and use leverage to press the target material with the pressure block. The pressure block swivels to change directions so that it is always in contact with the target. This jig really speeds up your work as you don't have to clamp the target material each time.

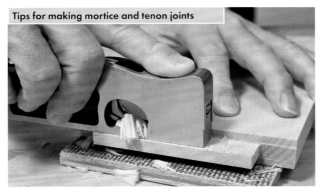

Tips for making mortice and tenon joints

Mortice jig

4 After completing the mortice holes, line things up and begin to fit the tenons. Leave the tenons a little on the tight side and then adjust with a planer until they can be inserted by hand. The lengths of both the mortice and tenon should be exactly the same so there won't be any rattling.

5 This jig is used to firmly press a piece of wood against the aluminium fence. It is super easy to use this jig to hold material firmly, or shift it as needed, while drilling. It was designed specifically to make continuous drilling much easier.

MORTICE THICKNESS

Generally, tenons should be a third of the thickness of the material. However, I tend to make mine about half the thickness. If the material in figure 1 on page 230 is 20mm thick, the length of the tenon will be 10mm, and the size of the longer glued face will be 5mm. On the other hand, the shorter (narrower) glued surface would only be about 3 to 5mm. The 'shoulders' left by these differences hide the gap so that the joint is cosmetically appealing. The mortice in figure 1 is rectangular in shape. This is what you get when you carve a mortice with a chisel – or a power tool called a square chisel. The mortice shown in figure 2 on page 230 uses a drill bit, so both ends are rounded as shown. Complete the accompanying tenon by chamfering the edges to match the rounded shape seen (see step 26 on page 237).

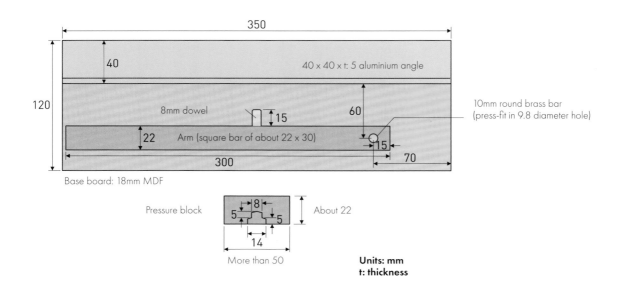

350
40
40 × 40 × t: 5 aluminium angle
120
8mm dowel
15
60
10mm round brass bar
(press-fit in 9.8 diameter hole)
22
Arm (square bar of about 22 × 30)
15
300
70
Base board: 18mm MDF

Pressure block
8
5
5
About 22
14
More than 50

Units: mm
t: thickness

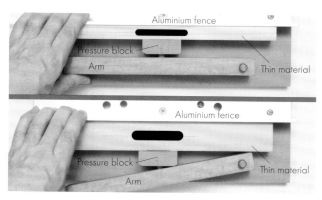

6 The dowel holes drilled in the pressure block are two-stage holes – that way, their heads can swivel. Even if the thickness of the material changes slightly, it can easily be held in place. Putting sandpaper on the front side of the pressure block will prevent slippage and hold the material much more securely.

7 This is a mortice jig comparison, viewed from directly above, with different thicknesses of wood in it. The swinging function of the pressure block allows the entire block surface to adhere to the target piece, even when wood thickness varies or the arm angle changes. The aluminium angle piece is used as a fence, so it needs to be firmly fixed to the base plate. In addition, the fence face must be perpendicular to the base plate. If adjustment is necessary, place a piece of paper, or something similar, between the base plate and the fence to make an accurate right angle. If the fence surface and mortice wall are not perfectly parallel, the joint will bend or warp when completed.

Mortice processing

8 Line up the tenon block to help determine the mortice location. The inner lines are 5mm from the outer lines and indicate mortice length.

9 Drill a hole in the centre of the wood. The first step is to drill both ends! The photo shows one end drilled. Next, it will be shifted and drilled on the other end.

10 Once both ends are drilled, open up the space between them. The trick is to slowly lower the bit. If the undrilled space between the holes is too narrow, the bit will bend at an angle, so leave the undrilled spaces a little wide.

11 Drill several holes between the initial holes and connect them together.

12 The mortice hole walls will be wavy. These waves are further cut down to flatten them out.

13 To position the hole in the centre, we flipped the material and shaved off any tiny deviations (you can see that the wood has been reversed because of the flipping).

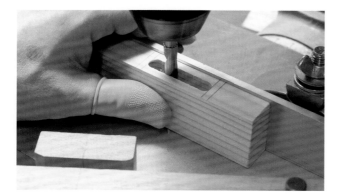

14 Once the mortice walls are almost flat you can move the piece side-to-side with the drill bit all the way down. This will smooth everything out. Use a rubber thumb cap to make it easier to manipulate the material.

Tenon processing

15 Once the mortice is made, the next step is to use the new-type vertical ripping guide to make the tenon. Hole length should be about 2mm shorter than its depth. Use calipers to measure both the material thickness and hole width. The formula is: **subtract the thickness of the tenon from the width of the hole = unnecessary part. Unnecessary part ÷ 2 = spacer thickness.**

16 Mark an O in the centre and an X on each wood edge. Sandwich a combination of spacers – of the required thickness – in the guide. Since we can still see an O in front of the spacer we need to follow the rule: **'If you can see the area marked with an O, insert a saw blade spacer'**. You can see the saw blade. Once the spacers are fully inserted we are ready to cut.

17 Make a vertical cut to the predetermined depth. The saw is the Japanese flush-cut straight-toothed version. Keep the saw horizontal and cut straight.

18 Once the cut is made on one side, flip the material over and clamp it again.

19 Cut the other side as well. The rules apply here too, so insert the saw blade spacer. The thickness of the tenon is now set.

20 Change the thickness of the spacer in your new-type ripping guide to 5mm and cut both ends of the mortice. The saw blade spacer is still sandwiched behind the material because there is a O visible.

21 The cuts have been made. Now it is time to cut out the tenons with the cross-cut guide.

22 Clamp the wood into the cross-cut guide and set the length hook. Once clamped, cut off the two unnecessary horizontal sections. After cutting off the horizontal parts (as seen), the saw blade can be turned vertically to cut off smaller unnecessary parts. Turn the material over and repeat.

CUTTING OUT THE MORTICE

If you make a jig like the one shown in the photo, you can cut off all four unwanted parts just by clamping once.

23 Tenon thickness is adjusted with a planer. The photo shows a shoulder plane being used to thin the tenon. The shoulder plane can also be used to adjust tenon shoulders if needed.

24 Both tenon ends are shaped with a box cutter to fit the rounded mortice sections. The tenon tip is also chamfered for ease of entry.

25 The mortice and tenon joint is complete. After gluing, correct any slight bumps with a jack plane. If the mortice must be drilled close to the material edge, it's best to still cut a 20mm long hole as before, and then just cut off any excess length after gluing.

26 If you want to make a rectangular mortice, carve both ends out with a chisel. This can be done easily with a block.

WOODEN PLUGS

This method involves driving a round bar through both the mortice and tenon to strengthen the joint. By slightly shifting the round bar hole positions, the two pieces will pull against each other when the round bar is driven in. This results in an extremely strong joint.

DUST COLLECTION PORT

Continually drilling with a drill press and/or mortice jig will produce a lot of wood chips. This can clog the hole you are drilling and obscure the tip from view. To solve this problem, we created a dust collection port that can be connected to a vacuum. Powerful magnets are embedded in the bottom of the unit so that it will stick firmly to the drill press worktable. The hose is just a drain hose from a washing machine. For the dust collection port, several square pieces of wood are laminated together to form a block, then two holes are drilled to form an L-shape. Use a drill bit that matches the hose's outer diameter.

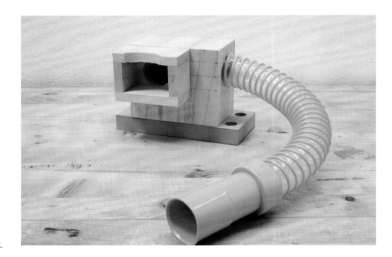

Set up behind a mortice hole jig.

The inside of the body has two holes that form an L-shape.

There are 12 strong magnets embedded in the bottom.

GLUING PLANKS TOGETHER AND HOMEMADE CLAMPS

In woodworking, there are methods for sanding and planing plank edges so that they can then be glued together to produce wider planks. For thin boards, as shown in the photo above right, sandwiching a piece of scrap wood between the two target boards will stabilize them for planing. In addition, to prevent misalignment we use F-type clamps across the entire seam, as shown in the photo above. This makes it much easier to sand after gluing.

Of course, we can only clamp as deeply as our clamps allow, but there is a method for determining the maximum width (pocket/depth) that can be reached with F-type clamps. Then, we just use less than that amount of material when gluing pieces together and repeat if necessary.

GLUING THIN PLANKS TOGETHER

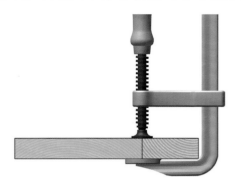

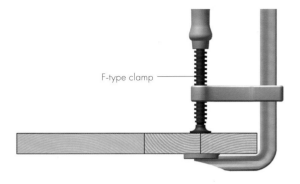

F-type clamp

Once the glue is dry, the same process can be repeated to make wider boards. F-type clamps are used to prevent misalignment, while the handmade clamps are used to firmly hold the adhesive surfaces together (handmade clamps not shown in diagram). This technique may not work in certain cases, but it could prove useful and is something all woodworkers should know.

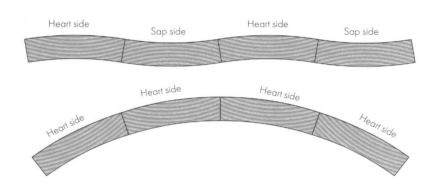

Heart side   Sap side   Heart side   Sap side

Heart side   Heart side   Heart side   Heart side

Warping

Boards tend to warp towards the sap side of the wood (the side closest to the bark), so it is easier to maintain a flat surface if you alternate the sap sides and heart sides (the side closest to the core) of your pieces when gluing. We also have to be conscious of planing direction, of course.

HOW TO MAKE YOUR OWN CLAMPS

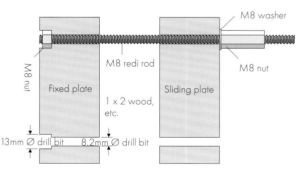

M8 washer

M8 nut

M8 redi rod

Fixed plate

Sliding plate

1 x 2 wood, etc.

13mm Ø drill bit   8.2mm Ø drill bit

M8 nut

Units: mm/Ø: diameter

1 This is how to produce handmade clamps using only M8 redi rod. We will use a drill press and mortice jig to make redi rod holes. If you don't have a jig, you can use a square piece of wood as a fence and attach it to the drill press worktable. With a jig, we must make sure that the surface against which the material to be drilled is pressed is perpendicular to the worktable. In both cases, scrap wood should be placed under the target piece to prevent tear out. A positioning stopper has been glued to the fence face so holes that are equidistant from the material ends can be drilled every time.

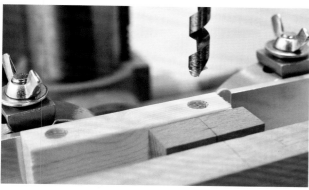

2 Drill two-stage holes in the fixed plate. First, drill a large hole with a 13mm bit that is about 15mm deep. Drill at both ends, with the material firmly up against the positioning stopper. Perform this process on all of the fixed plates at once.

3 Next, drill through holes with an 8.2mm drill bit.

4 Drill 8.2mm through holes in the sliding plates as well.

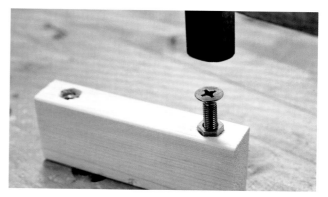

5 Thread a screw onto the M8 nut and then tap the nut into the sliding plate hole. Remove the screw and then repeat the process for all four holes and you're done.

SAW GUIDE FOR SET-SAW BLADE

This is a guide for 'set-saws', meaning saws where the kerf spreads so there is a 'set' gap behind the kerf. Although they are less accurate than straight-toothed blades, set-saws are often better for ripping. When ripping with a set-saw you can use a guide with embedded magnets to make straight cuts.

A magnetic sheet would scratch your set-saw so we'll embed strong, round magnets this time. The magnets are countersunk 1 to 2mm below the guide surface so they won't damage your set-saw.

With use the guide surface will become damaged, but don't worry, you can just use a planer to repair it. It doesn't matter if you can't fix the guide with a right-angle planer. The idea is to rough cut the piece and then plane it to a right angle. Be aware that whenever you repair the guide you'll be planing away tiny portions of its surface, so you will need to use a custom punch to push the magnets into their holes after each repair.

The guide length is up to you, but guide dimensions in the photo are 670 × 55 × 28mm (oak). The magnet holes are 30mm deep and 30mm apart, with an approximate diameter of 13mm.

HOW TO USE

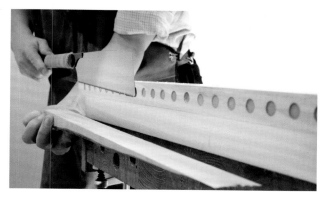

1 Here, a long piece of wood, a furniture leg, is being tapered vertically. A straight-toothed blade would produce a cleaner cut, and risk scarring the guide less, but the set-saw really cuts well.

2 You can see here that the guide surface has been scratched by the set-saw blade. The same is actually true for the surface we just cut.

3 Even if the cut surface is rough, this can be easily cleaned up with a planer.

4 If the guide surface gets damaged, it can be planed down as well.

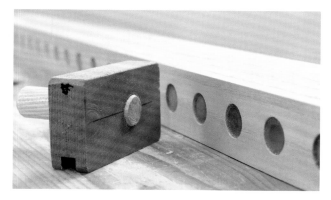

5 After finishing the guide surface with a planer, use a punch to push in the magnets. That way, the guide can be used for a long time. You can also adjust magnet strength by pushing the magnets in deeper.

6 When you're finished, place the punch into a hole without a magnet so you don't lose it.

TAIL GUIDE AND SAW BLADE SPACER WITH BEVEL

These two tools are useful for cutting box joints (splicing). The tail guide aids the blade when cutting at right angles and perpendicularly. You can use the guide by itself or in combination with a saw blade spacer and bevel.

This particular saw blade spacer is the same thickness as the saw, but the end has a sharpened, bevelled edge for gripping. Here, a replacement Pipe Saw Flat 225 blade is used. The wood is being cut with a Japanese flush-cut straight-toothed saw of the same thickness. The scribed lines are not pencilled. Rather, they are fine scratches that can help with precise cutting by placing the bevelled spacer in them. Then, when you apply the tail guide the spacer will be upright and in the exact cutting position and it becomes just a matter of removing the spacer and cutting. Thanks to these spacers, the guide can be reliably positioned and the user doesn't have to rely on visual measurements.

Tail guide

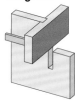

There is a magnetic sheet attached so that the material can be cut at right angles and perpendicular to the target.

Saw blade spacer with bevel

Use a saw blade spacer of the same thickness as the blade used to cut the wood. Sand a bevel in the end. Mark with an O on one side and an X on the other.

BASIC USAGE FOR BOX JOINTS

1 This piece is cut into five pieces. The tail guide is used to make perfect cuts.

2 The tail guide is placed on the wood as shown. The black material is the magnetic sheet.

3 Affix a depth stop to the saw blade when using the tail guide. In the photo, the tail guide is set so that the stabilizing tab will be visible for the camera.

4 This is a picture of the tail guide with the stabilizing tab on the operator's side. The tail guide can be used from either side.

TAIL GUIDE DIMENSIONAL DRAWING

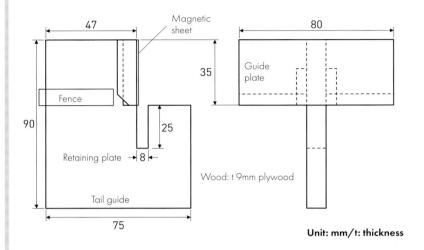

Magnetic sheet

47

Fence

90

Retaining plate

8

Tail guide

75

25

35

Guide plate

80

Wood: t 9mm plywood

Unit: mm/t: thickness

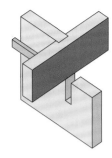

These dimensions are for reference only. You can make this tool as large as you feel is comfortable.

TAIL GUIDE PRODUCTION SEQUENCE

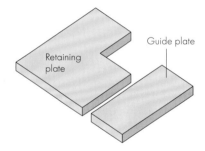

Retaining plate

Guide plate

1 Cut out from 9mm plywood (see step 1 opposite).

2 Cut a 3mm-deep groove in the guide plate (see step 2 opposite).

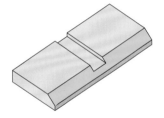

3 Chamfer the lower edge of the guide plate by about 5 x 5mm (see step 8 on page 248).

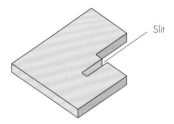

Slit

4 Cut a slit in the retaining plate for the saw blade to pass through (see step 9 on page 248).

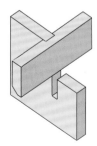

5 Glue the guide plate in place. Then attach the fence with double-sided tape (see step 13 on page 249).

HOW TO MAKE A TAIL GUIDE

1 Cut plates out of 9mm plywood (see step 1 opposite).

2 Cut a groove in the guide plate to fit the retaining plate. The two cuts that will become the groove are set using the cross-cut guide and calipers. Add 0.6mm (the saw blade thickness), then clamp at that position (see step 2 opposite).

3 Make the first cut. A brass depth stop is affixed at 3mm.

4 Now, re-clamp the material after shifting the board the proper distance using calipers.

5 The second cut has been made and the groove width is now fixed. The space between the two cuts will now become the groove.

6 Cut a few extra notches so that grooving will be easier.

7 Use a router plane to cut out the groove. The depth should be 3mm.

8 Once the grooving is done, the bottom edge of the guide plate is chamfered to make it easier to tilt. Although not introduced here, the 5 × 5mm groove allows for the guide to be tilted to produce dovetail joints (see step 3 on page 246).

9 Make a slit in the retaining plate for the saw blade to pass through. Set the guide plate in place and mark a cut line (see step 4 on page 246).

10 Clamp the wood in the cross-cut guide and make the first cut. Make sure the saw blade is upright.

11 Make a second incision about 8mm away from the first.

12 Use a box cutter or chisel to cut out the unnecessary tab.

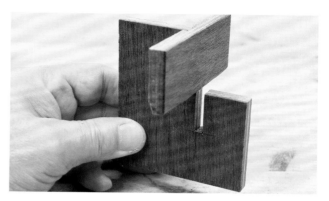

13 Apply glue to the groove and fix the guide plate to the retaining plate. Use a square to make sure that they are at right angles. Use a rubber band and a popsicle stick to add tension to the guide plate (see step 5 on page 246).

14 The two members are now glued together at right angles.

15 Use a square to attach a small fence, at right angles, to the guide plate with double-sided tape.

SAW BLADE SPACER WITH BEVELLED EDGE

Make this spacer from a blade that is the same thickness as your saw. The spacer in the photo is 'Flat', meaning a set-saw thickness: 0.6mm. It has been cut short with a pair of tin snips and bevelled to look like a planer blade. 'Single-edged blade' refers to a bevelled blade, sharpened at an angle on one side. It's shaped by angling the saw blade and grinding it on sandpaper. Put an X on this side and an O on the other. The flat side, marked with an O, is called the 'back side'. White vinyl tape is applied to the X side to adjust the looseness/tightness of the fit when sawing. See page 123 for more.

The saw blades on the left and centre of the photo are both 0.6mm thick. On the far right is a bevelled saw blade spacer cut from a Pipe Saw HI Flat 225.

See page 244 for instructions. For use see page 123.

TAPERED SLIDING DOVETAIL JOINT

The name of this joint may vary depending on the grain direction of the wood to be processed. It is variously called a 'tapered sliding joint' or 'sliding dovetail joint'. Here we call it a tapered sliding dovetail joint.

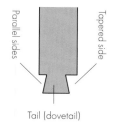

Tail (dovetail)

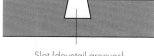

Slot (dovetail grooves)

In this section, we introduce a processing method in which the tail and pin are not parallel, but rather tapered. We call it a 'tapered sliding dovetail joint'. This joint is very strong because of the wedge effect created by the tapering. If produced properly this joint gives boxes, and other items, high strength and exceptional durability.

I nicknamed the jig the 'SD Jig' (sliding dovetail jig). The tail (convex) is machined first, and then the pin (groove/concave) is machined to match. Tail length and groove depth is 5mm. Also, one side of the tail is parallel, while the other is tapered.

When fitting, use a mallet to gently tap the joint. The thicker the spacer used, the tighter the fit between the tail and slot. The thinner the spacer, the looser the fit.

PROCESSING PROCEDURE

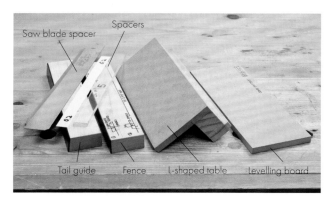

1 The tail guide and fence are covered with magnetic sheets. The L-shaped table can be substituted with an aluminium angle. Spacers can be combined for the right thickness. Saw blade spacers are the same thickness as the saw blade to be used.

2 Clamp the L-shaped table and levelling board onto the edge of the target piece. The edge and L-shaped table surface should be flush.

3 After clamping the L-shaped table to the wood, you can remove the (blue) clamps and levelling board.

4 Place the tail guide on the L-shaped table and clamp. This will determine the initial in-feed position. Note the tail guide incline (pencil marks show the angle). The magnetic sheet surface will now be set parallel to the wood edge.

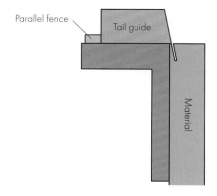

5 This is an illustration of photo 4. Clamp the tail guide tight against the parallel fence. Set the tail guide so that the cut direction is as shown in the figure.

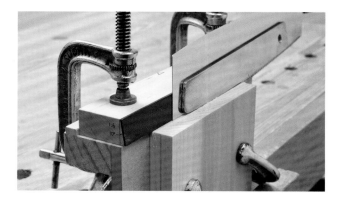

6 Set the depth stop to 5mm and cut.

7 Remove the tail guide. This cut runs parallel to the board width, while the opposite cut tapers (see pages 260–263 for illustrations).

8 Make an incision on the outer side then turn the tail guide over in order to reverse the slope. Use double-sided tape instead of clamps, place the material at a slight angle and press. This is the taper. Which one to make thinner will be determined by the work.

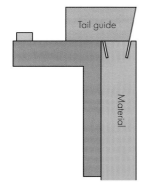

Tail guide

Material

9 This illustration represents photo 8. Flip the tail guide over, fix it (with a slight taper) using double-sided tape, then cut.

10 Make a cut.

11 You can see that the cut closest to us is tapered.

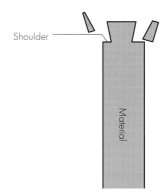

Shoulder

Material

12 The next step is to cut off the unnecessary wings as shown in the figure.

13 Clamp the L-shaped table to the workbench and place the material on top of both the L-shaped table and the levelling board.

14 Clamp the fence and the 5mm spacer against the L-shaped table. At this point, clamp the fence with the magnetic sheet side facing the spacer.

15 Remove the 5mm spacer.

16 Attach the saw blade to the magnetic sheet and cut. Use the depth stop at 5mm, but don't rely on it to perfectly remove the unwanted part as the cut depth is not 5mm on the tapered side. Do not cut too deep.

17 Cut off the unnecessary part. The piece is tapered, as you can see from the cut-off.

18 Cut off the other, parallel, side in the same way. We now have a tail with a length of 5mm. Put a red line on the non-tapered (parallel) side to distinguish it from the tapered side. (Instructions continue on page 256.)

HOW TO GET A GOOD VIEW OF THE CUT-OUT SHOULDER SURFACE

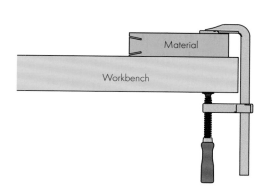

1 Fix the material to the workbench.

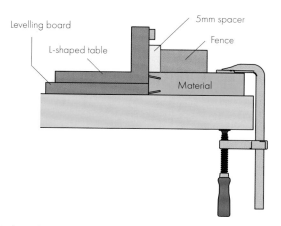

2 Place the 5mm spacer between the fence and the L-shaped table – which is on the levelling board. Fix the fence to the material with clamps or double-sided tape.

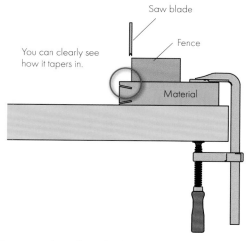

3 Removing the L-shaped table, levelling board and 5mm spacer will allow you to see the portion of the body (the circle part) to be cut out. This will help prevent overcutting (see picture opposite).

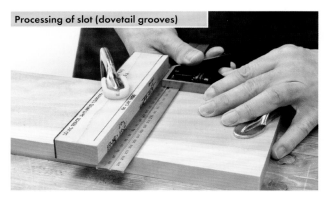

19 Place a square on the surface opposite the magnetic sheet. Clamp the fence in place and draw a pencil line at that position. Also, draw a line on the fence 5–6mm from the back edge. This will serve as a boundary beyond which we will not clamp.

20 Place the saw blade spacer and plastic spacer against the fence. The saw blade spacer is the same thickness as our saw blade (a Japanese flush-cut straight-toothed replacement blade). Here we will use a Pipe Saw Flat 225.

21 Place the spacers between the tail guide and the fence and fix with a clamp or double-sided tape. The magnetic sheet on the tail guide is oriented with the taper down, as shown in the picture.

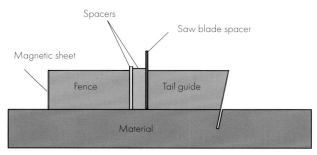

22 This is an illustration of photo 21. Fix the fence to the material. At this point, the magnetic sheet is facing out. Fix spacers and the saw blade spacer between the tail guide.

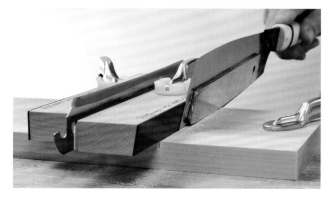

23 The first cut has been made and one side of the groove (the parallel side) is now cut.

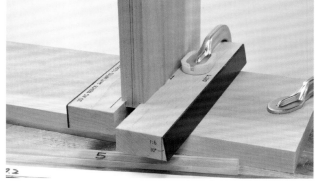

24 Leave the fence in place and remove the spacers and the tail guide. Flip the tail guide to change the inclination direction and pinch the tail of the dovetail. The parallel tail section is against the fence. Make sure that both edges of the tail board line up with both edges of the slot board or your taper width will be off.

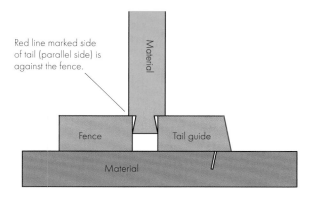

Red line marked side of tail (parallel side) is against the fence.

Material

Fence   Tail guide

Material

25 This is an illustration of photo 24. Leave the fence in place, remove the spacers and the tail guide. Flip the tail guide and sandwich the completed dovetail section in place. The red line (parallel side) of the dovetail should be on the fence side.

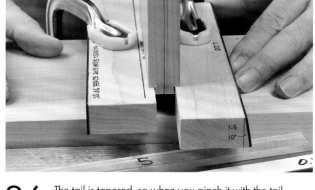

26 The tail is tapered, so when you pinch it with the tail guide, the guide will also taper. The tail guide slope is opposite to the first time. The border drawn on the fence is where the shoulder of the tail should be placed (see step 19 opposite).

27 The second incision can now be made. The groove width is now correct.

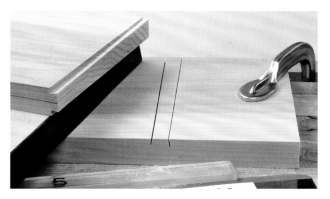

28 You can see that the near end of the two incisions is slightly narrower.

29 Use the original tail length to set the router plane depth. As we have done before, set up the fence to make two cuts inside the tail groove. Be sure to add a 1mm spacer under the fence so the cuts aren't too deep.

30 Press the router plane cutter into the pin board side to make small cuts. Make two of these cuts, both to a depth of approximately 5mm. Make sure the cuts connect with the widest point at the bottom of the tail groove (see photo). This will reduce tear out.

31 Insert a paint scraper and tilt it to the side to break off the fins inside the tail groove.

32 Use the router plane to finish the groove bottom to the predetermined depth.

33 Draw a red line on the parallel side of the completed groove to distinguish it from the tapered side.

Fitting

34 Gently insert the tail into the groove with both red lines on the same side. Once the tail stops, mark the pin board's edge position on the tail board with a pencil (circled).

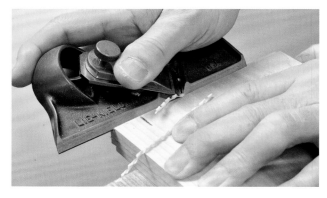

35 You can now adjust the tail width bit-by-bit with a planer. You can use a chisel or sandpaper to make adjustments instead of a planer, if you wish. Repeat this adjustment several times as necessary.

36 Instead of using a planer, a dovetail-shaped groove can be cut out of a block as shown in the photo. Then, thin strips of sandpaper can be attached to the area marked with a red line using double-sided tape. This sanding block can now be used to adjust the fit of the dovetail.

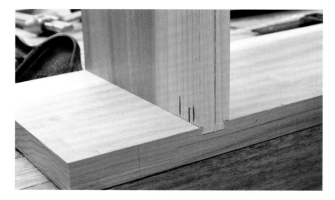

37 Lastly, give the dovetail a tap with a mallet. The pencil lines show that the work was finished with just two adjustments. It's useful to measure the distance between the tail material centre and the fence line drawn in step 19 on page 256 to help position the tail board. This is called the offset distance.

SLIDING DOVETAIL JIG

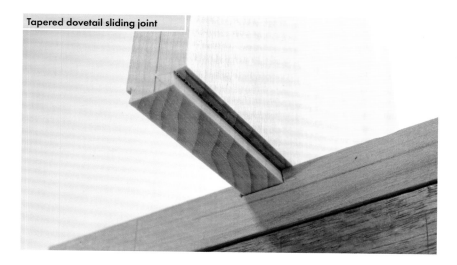

Tapered dovetail sliding joint

This jig is designed to make hand tool use easier when making dovetail joints, which are not easy to make, even with power tools.

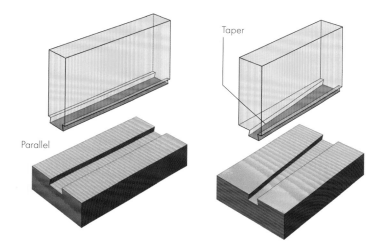

Taper

Parallel

This joint has two types: parallel and tapered. The tapered type becomes stronger and stronger as it is hammered in due to the wedge effect and, although sliding dovetail jigs can be processed in both ways, this book uses the tapered type. Please refer to pictures and cross-sectional drawings in this section for the L-shaped guide parts you need to make. Aside from the guide itself the parts are pretty simple, so we won't give specific instructions for them.

Inclined cuts can actually be made by placing a thin square bar under some angle material with a magnetic sheet attached. The important thing is how to determine the thickness of the spacer. This will be explained in detail on page 263.

TAPERED SLIDING DOVETAIL JOINT PRODUCTION SEQUENCE

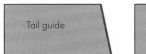 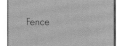

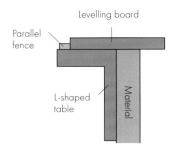

1 Attach the magnetic sheets to the tail guide and the fence. The tail guide is used to machine the tails and slots for dovetail joints.

2 Clamp the L-shaped table and the levelling board together and place on the material. Then clamp the L-shaped table to the material. The levelling board must be flush with the L-shaped table surface.

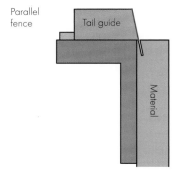

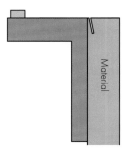

3 Remove the levelling board and clamp the tail guide against the parallel fence. Cut to a depth of 5mm, paying attention to the inclination.

4 Make a 5mm deep cut that runs parallel to the width of the material edge. Remove the tail guide.

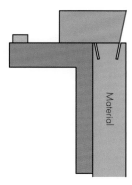

5 Invert the tail guide and fix it on the material with double-sided tape so that the cut tapers at one end. Now, cut. Be careful not to make the taper too thin! If it's too thin the router plane blade won't fit in the dovetail grooving later on.

6 Cuts have now been made on both the material edges. In this case the left side of the cut is parallel, and the right side is tapered.

Machining the slot

Parallel side — Tapered side

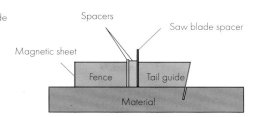

Spacers

Saw blade spacer

Magnetic sheet

7 Cut off the unnecessary parts of the tail.

8 Finished tail.

9 Fix the fence to the material, magnetic sheet side out. Insert spacers and the saw blade spacer, fix the tail guide and cut.

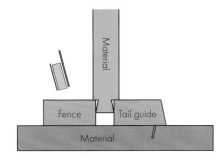

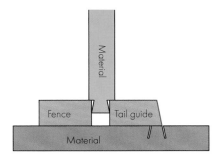

10 Remove all spacers and the tail guide. Leave the fence in place. Now pinch the tail of the dovetail between the tail guide and the fence. Be aware that you must flip the tail guide to change the slope direction.

11 Determine the width of the slot (dovetail groove) and make the required outside cut. Remove the fence and the tail guide.

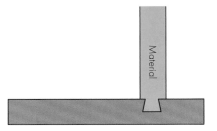

12 Remove the unnecessary material from inside the groove with a router plane.

13 Adjust the fit and complete the tapered dovetail sliding joint.

PRINCIPLES OF THE SLIDING DOVETAIL JIG

Turning over the tail guide allows us to cut both tails (dovetail)
and slots (dovetail grooves).

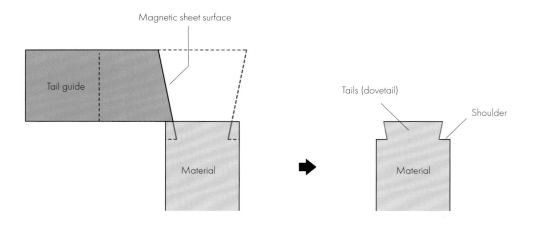

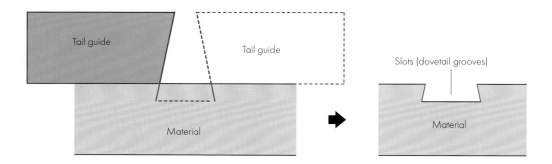

The most important principle of the sliding dovetail jig is
that it can form reversible dovetail-shaped inclines simply
by changing the direction of the tail guide. For more detailed
information on how to use the sliding dovetail jig, please
refer to page 251.

CROSS-SECTIONAL VIEW OF EACH SLIDING DOVETAIL JIG PART

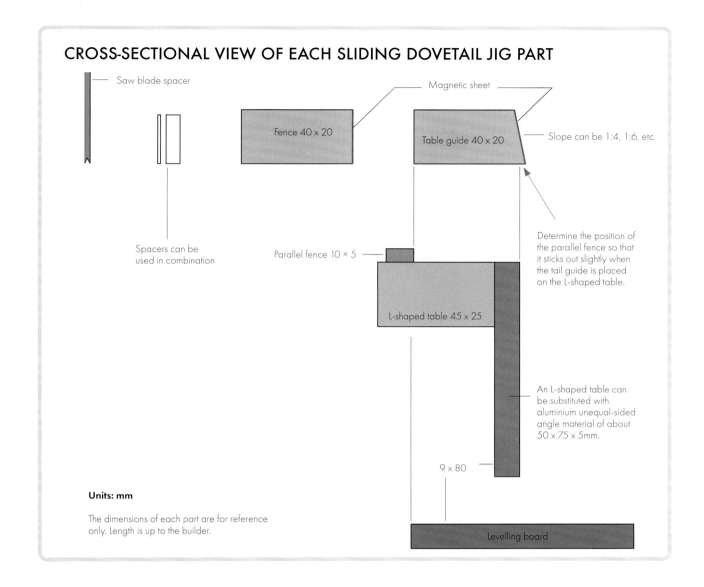

Saw blade spacer

Spacers can be used in combination

Magnetic sheet

Fence 40 x 20

Table guide 40 x 20

Slope can be 1:4, 1:6, etc.

Determine the position of the parallel fence so that it sticks out slightly when the tail guide is placed on the L-shaped table.

Parallel fence 10 × 5

L-shaped table 45 x 25

An L-shaped table can be substituted with aluminium unequal-sided angle material of about 50 x 75 x 5mm.

9 × 80

Units: mm

The dimensions of each part are for reference only. Length is up to the builder.

Levelling board

Determine spacer thickness

Once you have completed all the components of your sliding dovetail jig, determine the length of the tail (i.e. slot depth) in order to determine the thickness of the sliding dovetail jig slider. In this book, tail length is always set at 5mm and spacers of appropriate thickness are used. This means that even if you use the same sliding dovetail jig, spacer thickness will vary depending on tail length. For example, you can prepare spacers that are 5mm long and 7mm long and use them according to need. The saw blade spacer should be the same thickness as the saw used. Here, a Japanese flush-cut straight-toothed saw is used for cutting, and a Pipe Saw Flat 225 of the same thickness is used as a saw blade spacer.

1 Attach the fence to a piece of scrap wood of the appropriate size.

2 The fence can be seen on the far right with the scrap wood pointing up. Place the tail guide against the fence. Place a ruler on the inclined surface (the magnetic sheet surface) and carve a line on the thick part of the end material. Turn the tail guide over and mark again to make a 'V' shaped line. The horizontal line we see is 5mm deep.

3 If you measure the distance at the base of the 5mm scribed line, you will have the basic spacer thickness. The same is true if we use a 7mm deep line. In practice, spacer thickness should be adjusted so that the fit is a little tight because we want to be forced to tap it slightly with the mallet.

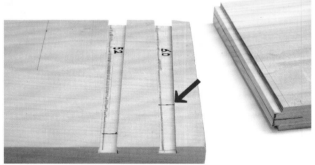

4 Changing spacer thickness changes groove width. If you insert the tail material seen on the right, from back to front, the amount that can be inserted will change. The pencil lines marked in the grooves indicate the furthest insertion position.

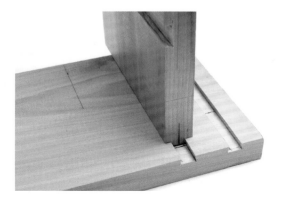

5 Here, the tail is inserted into the groove on the left. You can see that the tail goes in about 80–90% of the way. In truth, it's safe to keep it at this stage and then simply adjust with a sanding block (see step 36 on page 258). Then, tap a little with a mallet. You can test thicker or thinner spacers for a tighter or looser fit. Change thickness several times and repeat the grooving process to find the best fit. Then, use that spacer for your actual production.

BENCH SEAT WITH TAPERED SLIDING DOVETAIL JOINT

Practise 'Tapered sliding dovetail joints' from page 251 by making a bench seat. This is where the sliding dovetail jig comes in. The depth of the joint and tail (i.e., the depth of the dovetail groove) is 5mm. The bench is made of 20mm thick yellow pine. Leg height is decided by actually sitting on the bench during the production process. The two legs have their parallel cut-outs on the inside, facing each other. The tapered sides are on the outside. This will provide enough space to work with the sliding dovetail jig. Also of note, the tail is wider at the back and narrower at the front, meaning the dovetails are inserted from back to front. Please see the following illustrations for more details.

BENCH SEAT DIMENSIONS

700

50

520

330 325

230

t:20

190

110 95

40

Units: mm/ t: thickness

BENCH SEAT PRODUCTION SEQUENCE

Parallel

R

a

1a Make a cut parallel to the edge (see step 4 on page 268).

Taper

R

b

1b Make a tapered cut on the opposite side (see step 5 on page 268).

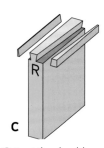

R

c

1c Cut out the shoulders (see step 8 on page 269).

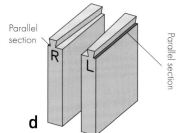

Parallel section

R L

Parallel section

d

1d Make two legs (see step 10 on page 269).

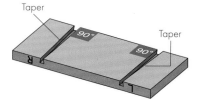

Taper

90°

Taper

90°

R

2 Slots (dovetail grooves) are cut into the back of the seat plate. The parallel parts from 1a fits into the 90-degree sections in the illustration. The tapered parts from 1b face the side labelled 'Taper' (see step 11 on page 269).

3 Cut 3mm deep grooves on three sides of the brace. The width of the grooves should be equal to the thickness of the legs (see step 20 on page 271).

Curve

4 Cut out the curved sections at both ends. This process can be done later (see step 30 on page 272).

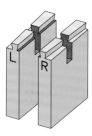

5 Make notches in the centre of the dovetailed legs for the brace (see step 23 on page 271).

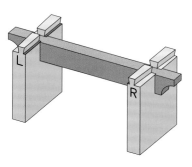

6 Assemble temporarily. Adjust the top of the brace so that it runs flush with the shoulders on the dovetailed pieces (see step 28 on page 272).

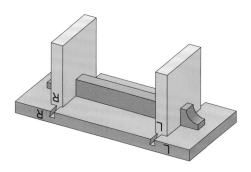

7 Temporarily assemble the seat plate as well (see step 29 on page 272).

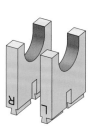

8 Cut curves in the legs (see step 32 on page 273).

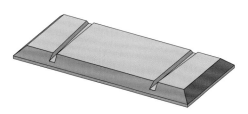

9 Carve a large chamfer around the bottom edge of the seat plate. Rough cut the chamfer with a scrub plane and then finish with a jack plane. Chamfer as seen (see step 35 on page 273).

10 Glue and it's finished.

MAKE A BENCH SEAT WITH A TAPERED SLIDING DOVETAIL JOINT

1 Cut out the seat board, legs and brace.

Tail cutting

2 This is the tailing process. Fix the L-shaped table surface flush with the leg end. Then, attach the levelling board to the L-shaped table. I'm not using clamps here because the levelling board has magnets embedded in it.

3 The L-shaped table has been clamped to the leg. The levelling board is removed to show that the table surface and the leg end are flush. This is the left leg, with the side facing us being the front.

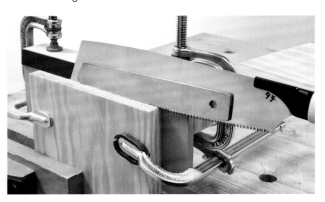

4 Set the tail guide and cut to a depth of 5mm. Attach the depth stop to the saw blade. This cut is parallel to the edge (see step 1a on page 266).

5 Next, we cut the other side. Turn the tail guide over, change the direction of inclination and fix it in a slightly tapered position with double-sided tape (see step 1b on page 266).

6 Cut the other leg in the same manner as described above.

7 Now, our two cuts have been made. In the photo, the far side of the left incision is slightly narrower. The cut on the right is parallel.

8 The next step is to cut the shoulders. Clamp the L-shaped table to the table. Use the levelling board as a sleeper. Butt the wood against the L-shaped table. Use the white 5mm spacer to set the cut depth (see step 1c on page 266).

9 Clamp the fence with the 5mm spacer held between it and the L-shaped table. Make sure the magnetic sheet is facing the spacer. Pull out the spacer and cut. You can leave the depth stop attached to your saw, but don't rely on it to make the cut.

10 The dovetails on the left and right legs are done. The thin cut-offs can be seen on top of the dovetails. Prevent mistakes by drawing a red line on the parallel side of the dovetail. See step 18 on page 254 and step 1d on page 266).

Processing dovetail grooves (slots)

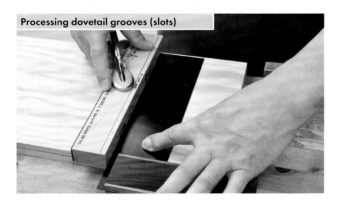

11 Fix the fence at the proper offset distance (see step 37 on page 258). It's hard to clamp the fence while placing the saw correctly, so the fence is attached with double-sided tape first and then clamped after. Don't forget that both legs must be parallel, so it's important to use a square (see step 2 on page 266).

12 This is the process for attaching the tail guide. Place the spacer(s), and the saw blade spacer, between the fence and the tail guide, then secure. Pay attention to the slanted face direction on the tail guide.

13 Here is the first cut. You can clearly see the tail guide's slanted face here.

14 Remove the tail guide and spacers, leaving the fence in place. Flip the tail guide to change the direction, then pinch the dovetail. The leg and seat plate width are different so the tail guide is fixed where the centre of both materials are aligned.

15 After making the two slanted cuts, we need to make a few more cuts so that the groove can be cleaned out more easily. Break out the groove waste with a paint scraper.

16 Set the depth of the router plane using the dovetail as a guide (see step 29 on page 257). Then, clean out the bottom of the groove.

17 Insert the legs into the grooves to dry fit.

18 If the fit is too tight, use a sanding block (see step 36 on page 258) to adjust. In the photo, the tail is being adjusted using an edge plane.

19 Finish the leg in the same manner as described above.

Making the brace

20 Notch the area where the legs fit on three sides. Use an Accurate Guide, etc., to copy the leg material thickness onto the brace and then cut to a depth of 3mm. Make several cuts between the edge cuts (see step 3 on page 266).

21 Carve out the groove waste with a router plane on all three sides. Leave the part that touches the seat board untouched.

22 Once the notches on one side are made, fit the notch into the leg and mark the other leg position.

23 Use the tail guide to cut the leg for the brace (see step 5 on page 267).

24 The cut width should be measured with calipers and copied onto the leg material.

25 Cut both sides and then remove the notch with a coping saw. I made a mistake with the dimensions here and it turned out to be too wide. I'll show you how to fix these types of mistakes next.

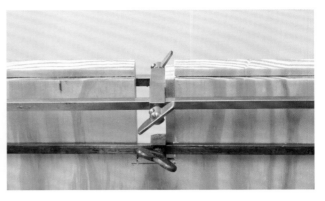

26 Fill in the difference from the correct dimension with a small piece of wood called a 'shim'. Use the new-type vertical ripping guide to cut out the correct size of shim and attach it below the shoulder. Use clamps to tightly glue it in place.

27 Once the corrections have been made, use a chisel to fix the roughly cut bottom.

28 Dry fit and check that the top of the brace is flush with the shoulders of the dovetails. Adjust if necessary (see step 6 on page 267).

29 Next, check the fit between the seat plate, brace and legs. Make sure the dovetails fit well (see step 7 on page 267).

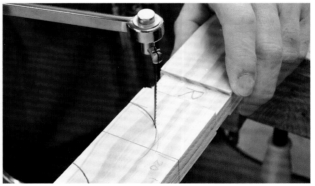

30 Use an empty spray can to draw lines for the decorative curves on the brace. Cut them out with a coping saw (see step 4 on page 266).

31 Finish the decorative curves by wrapping sandpaper around the can used for marking and sand as necessary.

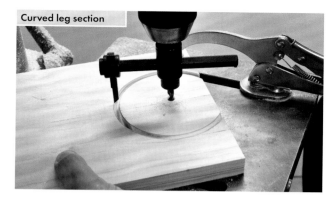

32 Process the U-shaped cuts in the legs with a circle cutter (as seen) or a hole saw. Cut down to half of the board thickness, then turn the material over and cut out the rest (see step 8 on page 267).

33 Use a chisel to straighten the cut-outs.

34 After that, finish with a spokeshave and sandpaper.

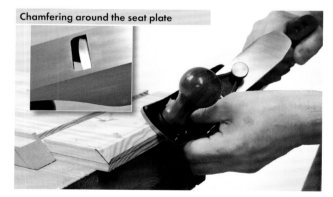

35 A large chamfer is made around the entire seat plate. I used a scrub plane for rough cutting because it works fast. The blade is curved and cuts narrow and deep. When chamfering, start with the end grain (see step 9 on page 267).

36 After rough cutting is complete, it's time for the fine finish. Glue down thin boards, to be used as fences, about 20mm away from the seat plate on the front and left side. You can achieve a beautiful finish by simply planing up to your marked line now.

37 The front and left sides have now been cleanly chamfered. As you can see, the thin fences form an L-shape. The seat plate should be held down with clamps. Flip the seat plate, fix it in the same position as before, and then cut the remaining short and long sides.

38 Our bench seat is now complete.

Beautiful chair and shelf with tapered dovetail joints.

SUPPLIERS

The following companies are a selection, rather than a complete list, where you can purchase Japanese flush-cut saws, and other tools and materials, similar to the ones used in this book.

UK

Axminster Tools
www.axminstertools.com

Charnwood
Charnwood.net

Misumi for Star-M tools/components
www.uk.misumi-ec.com

Mititoyo UK Ltd
www.mitutoyo.co.uk

Starrett UK
www.starrett.co.uk

Workshop Heaven Fine Tools
www.workshopheaven.com

Yandles
www.yandles.co.uk

Canada

Lee Valley Tools
www.leevalley.com

US

William Fehrenbach
wjfbach@gmail.com

Hida Tool & Hardware Co.
www.hidatool.com

Highland Woodworking
www.highlandwoodworking.com

Lie-Nielsen Toolworks Inc
www.lie-nielsen.com

Pony Jorgensen
www.ponyjorgensen.com

Rockler Woodworking and Hardware
www.rockler.com

Woodcraft
www.woodcraft.com

Japan

ARM Sangyo.Co.Ltd
www.armsangyo.co.jp

Mirai Jigs and Fixtures
www.mirai-tokyo.co.jp
This is the author's website. The saw, MIRAI Alpha 265 Flush Cut Pull Saw Blade, used in this book and other saw guides can be purchased here.

ZetSaw, by Okada Hardward Mfg.Co., Ltd, Japan
www.z-saw.co.jp/en/

METRIC TO IMPERIAL CONVERSION CHART

2mm ($\frac{5}{64}$in)	60mm ($2\frac{3}{8}$in)	210mm ($8\frac{1}{4}$in)	840mm (33in)
3mm ($\frac{1}{8}$in)	63mm ($2\frac{1}{2}$in)	215mm ($8\frac{1}{2}$in)	865mm (34in)
4mm ($\frac{5}{32}$in)	65mm ($2\frac{5}{8}$in)	220mm ($8\frac{3}{4}$in)	890mm (35in)
6mm ($\frac{1}{4}$in)	70mm ($2\frac{3}{4}$in)	230mm (9in)	915mm (36in)
7mm ($\frac{9}{32}$in)	75mm (3in)	235mm ($9\frac{1}{4}$in)	940mm (37in)
8mm ($\frac{5}{16}$in)	80mm ($3\frac{1}{8}$in)	240mm ($9\frac{1}{2}$in)	965mm (38in)
9mm ($\frac{11}{32}$in)	85mm ($3\frac{1}{4}$in)	250mm ($9\frac{3}{4}$in)	990mm (39in)
10mm ($\frac{3}{8}$in)	90mm ($3\frac{1}{2}$in)	255mm (10in)	1015mm (40in)
11mm ($\frac{7}{16}$in)	93mm ($3\frac{2}{3}$in)	257mm ($10\frac{1}{8}$in)	1040mm (41in)
12mm ($\frac{1}{2}$in)	95mm ($3\frac{3}{4}$in)	280mm (11in)	1065mm (42in)
13mm ($\frac{1}{2}$in)	100mm (4in)	305mm (12in)	1090mm (43in)
14mm ($\frac{9}{16}$in)	105mm ($4\frac{1}{8}$in)	330mm (13in)	1120mm (44in)
15mm ($\frac{9}{16}$in)	110mm ($4\frac{1}{4}$–$4\frac{3}{8}$in)	355mm (14in)	1145mm (45in)
16mm ($\frac{5}{8}$in)	115mm ($4\frac{1}{2}$in)	380mm (15in)	1170mm (46in)
17mm ($\frac{11}{16}$in)	120mm ($4\frac{3}{4}$in)	405mm (16in)	1195mm (47in)
18mm ($\frac{23}{32}$in)	125mm (5in)	430mm (17in)	1220mm (48in)
19mm ($\frac{3}{4}$in)	130mm ($5\frac{1}{8}$in)	460mm (18in)	1245mm (49in)
20mm ($\frac{3}{4}$in)	135mm ($5\frac{1}{4}$n)	485mm (19in)	1270mm (50in)
21mm ($\frac{13}{16}$in)	140mm ($5\frac{1}{2}$in)	510mm (20in)	1295mm (51in)
22mm ($\frac{7}{8}$in)	145mm ($5\frac{3}{4}$in)	535mm (21in)	1320mm (52in)
23mm ($\frac{29}{32}$in)	150mm (6in)	560mm (22in)	1345mm (53in)
24mm ($\frac{15}{16}$in)	155mm ($6\frac{1}{8}$in)	585mm (23in)	1370mm (54in)
25mm (1in)	160mm ($6\frac{1}{4}$in)	610mm (24in)	1395mm (55in)
30mm ($1\frac{1}{8}$in)	165mm ($6\frac{1}{2}$in)	635mm (25in)	1420mm (56in)
32mm ($1\frac{1}{4}$in)	170mm ($6\frac{3}{4}$in)	660mm (26in)	1450mm (57in)
35mm ($1\frac{3}{8}$in)	178mm ($6\frac{7}{8}$in)	685mm (27in)	1475mm (58in)
38mm ($1\frac{1}{2}$in)	180mm (7in)	710mm (28in)	1500mm (59in)
40mm ($1\frac{5}{8}$in)	185mm ($7\frac{1}{4}$in)	735mm (29in)	1525mm (60in)
45mm ($1\frac{3}{4}$in)	190mm ($7\frac{1}{2}$in)	760mm (30in)	
50mm (2in)	195mm ($7\frac{3}{4}$in)	785mm (31in)	
55mm ($2\frac{1}{8}$–$2\frac{1}{4}$in)	200mm (8in)	815mm (32in)	

Measurements

The measurements in this book are stated in millimetres, which can be converted to inches using the chart above. It is good practice to choose one or the other rather than use a mix of metric and imperial.

Safety

Woodworking is inherently dangerous. Improper use of tools, especially power tools, and disregard for safety, can lead to serious injury or death. The publisher accepts no responsibility for anyone's safety when using this book. Take extra care when working. If you don't feel it's safe for you to perform the techniques described in this book, don't do them until you receive the proper training.

Restrictions

The unique jigs, guides, tools and equipment introduced in this book were invented by the author, Toyohisa Sugita. There is no restriction on readers creating their own similar items and using them for personal enjoyment. However, commercializing or selling them without permission is strictly prohibited.

ABOUT THE AUTHOR

Small cruising yacht built by Toyohisa Sugita.

Toyohisa Sugita is a woodwork researcher and DIY advisor. He was born in 1951 in Tokyo and at the age of 28 began building his own 8.4m cruising yacht. He completed and launched this wonderful vessel at the age of 33. The yacht was the starting point for his woodworking research. Sugita works in the development, manufacturing and sales of woodworking products as well as in the production and sales of woodworking DVDs. In addition, he is involved as a distributor for Lie-Nielsen Western planers and Wood River Western planers.

Books related to his unique woodworking methods include: *Sugita Woodworking Method*; *All About Woodworking* (Ohmsha), *Super Epoch-making Woodworking Techniques* (Studio Tac Creative), and *The Ultimate Art of Trimming* (Graphic-sha Publishing). He is also the co-author of *Routers & Trimmers for Authentic Woodworking: The Definitive Edition!* and *A Book for Enjoying Weekend Woodworking* (both published by Gakken Plus). For this book, he was also in charge of the three-dimensional computer graphics, including shooting step-by-step photographs and generating figures for schematics. He loves the opportunity to speak with anyone about woodworking and the techniques presented in this book.

INDEX

A

Accurate Guide
    accessories 215–219
    making 203–208
    principles/use of 193–194, 209
adhesives 36
adjustable squares 36
aluminium ripping guides 20
angle correction 181
angles 36, 181

B

bandages 36
bench hooks 163
bench seat with tapered sliding dovetail
    joints 265–274
blades
    cutting off toe 31
    protecting 35
    replacement 29
bottom board rabbets, hiding 126–130
box cutters 36
boxes
    case mitre joint 105–115
    drawers 153–159
    finger-jointed with lid 138–146
    five interlocking pins box joint 116–125
    frame and panel joint 147–152
    hiding bottom board rabbets 126–130
    holding rods 216
    Hon-Inro mechanism 105, 131
    rabbet joint 100–104, 131–137
    reinforcing with splines 213–214
    Tsuke-Inro mechanism 105, 131
    using mitre planing table 167
bridle joints 89–91
burrs, preventing 30

C

C-shape clamps 39
calculators 36
calipers 36, 37–38
candles 28, 36
case mitre cutting guides 220–229
case mitre joint boxes 105–115

chips, preventing 30
chisel guides 125
chiselling joints, without a rabbet 130
clamps
    making 240–241
    types 39
combination squares 36
conversion tables 276
coping saws 29
craft sticks 36
cross-cut guides 21–24
cross-cutting 13
cut-depth, setting 30–31
cut-off capture trays 24
cutting ends of wood 34
cutting with hand saws 32–33

D

datum lines 34, 35
decorative edges 181–182
depth stops 9
drawers 153–159
dust collection ports 238

F

F-type clamps 39, 239
finger-jointed boxes with lid 138–146
five interlocking pins box joint 120–125
flush-cut saws 9, 29
flush-cut, straight-toothed Japanese saws
    9, 29
four-way speed clamps 39
frame and panel joint boxes 147–152
framing techniques
    bridle joint frame 87–91
    grooved bridle joint frame 92–97
    grooves within the rabbet 60
    half lap joint photo frame 42–51
    holding rods 216
    mitre jointed frames 183–185
    mitred half lap joint photo frame 71–77
    mitred half lap joint with groove or
        rabbeted frame 78–86
    rabbeted half lap joint photo frame
        52–60

reinforcing with splines 210–212
    splined mitre joint photo frame 61–70

G

glue 36
gluing clamps 39
gluing, planks 239–240
grooved bridle joints 94–97
grooving guides 193–194, 203–209,
    215–219

H

half lap joint lattices 198–202
half lap joints 44–51
hand planes 9
hand saws
    cutting with 32–33
    handles 27
    holding 32
    replacement blades 29, 31
    setting cut depth 30
    troubleshooting 28
    types 9, 29, 275
    using with magnetic guides 28
hand tools, advantages 6
handles, saws 27
handscrew clamps 39
holding hand saws 32
holding rods 216
Hon-Inro mechanism 105, 131
housing joints 195–197

I

imperial measurement conversion tables
    276
Inro boxes 105, 131
instant glue 36

J

Japanese saws 9, 29, 275
joining 13

K

knives 36

L

length hooks 25–26

lid frame grooving 145

M

magnetic guides, sawing with 28

marking gauges 36

marking wood 35

measurements 9, 276

measuring tapes 36

measuring wood 34

metric to imperial conversion tables 276

mitre cutting guides, with T-shaped stopper 172–185

mitre jigs 168–171

mitre jointed frames 183–185

mitre planing tables 165, 167

mitred half lap joints 73–77

mitred half lap joints with groove or rabbeted frames 80–86

mitred inset panels 92–97

mortice and tenon joints 230–238

N

new-type ripping guides 18–20

non-set tooth saws 29

O

one-shot cutting 9

P

panels

mitred inset 92–97

raised 86

pencils 36

photo frames

bridle joint 87–91

grooved bridle joint 92–97

half-lap joint 42–51

mitred half lap joint 71–77

mitred half lap joint with groove or rabbeted frame 78–86

rabbeted half lap joint 52–60

splined mitre joint 61–70

pistol-grip handles 27

planing tables, mitre 165, 167

planks, gluing 239–240

protractors 36

R

rabbet joint boxes 100–104, 131–137

rabbeted half lap joints 54–60

rabbeting guides 18, 186–192

rails 43

raised panels 86

reinforcing with splines 210–214

right-angle and width planers 166

ripping guides

aluminium 20

building 17, 19–20

new-type 18–20

processing wood with 13

rabbet 18

using 12–16

rubbers 36

rulers 36

S

sanding blocks 9

saw blade spacers with bevels 125, 244, 245, 250

saw guides for set-saw blades 242–243

sawdust catchers 14

saws

cutting with 32–33

handles 27

holding 32

replacement blades 29, 31

setting cut depth 30

troubleshooting 28

types 9, 29, 275

using with magnetic guides 28

set-saw blades guide 242–243

set-tooth saws 29

setting cut depth 30–31

shooting boards 162, 164

sliding dovetail jigs 259–264

sliding dovetail joints 251–264, 265–274

speed squares 36

splined mitre joints 61–70

splines, reinforcing with 210–214

spring clamps 39

squares 36

stabilizing tools 39

stiles 43

straight handles, saws 27

straight-toothed blades 27

Sugita woodworking method (overview) 6, 8–9

suppliers 275

T

T-shaped stoppers 175, 179–180

tail guides 244–249

tape measures 36

tapered sliding dovetail joints 251–264, 265–274

tapered sliding joints 251–264, 265–274

tenons 150–152

toe of blade, cutting off 31

tools

advantages of hand tools 6

calipers 36, 37–38

clamps 39, 240–241

cross-cut guides 21–24

hand saws 27–35

length hooks 25–26

miscellaneous 36–37

ripping guides 12–20

for stabilizing 39

Tsuke-Inro mechanism 105, 131

U

utility knives 36

W

web clamps 39

wood

choosing 34

preparing 34–35

wooden plugs 238

woodworking glue 36

First designed and published in Japan by Graphic-sha Publishing Co. Ltd, 2021
© 2021 Toyohisa Sugita,
© 2021 Graphic-sha Publishing Co. Ltd
Book design: Katsuharu Takahashi (eats & crafts)
Editing support: Yuka Tsuchida
Photography: Takayuki Yoshizaki (chapter openers) and Toyohisa Sugita (step-by-step sequences)
3D illustrations: Toyohisa Sugita
Proofreading: ZERO-MEGA CO., LTD.
Editing: Naoko Yamamoto (Graphic-sha Publishing)
Foreign edition production and management: Takako Motoki (Graphic-sha Publishing)

This English edition published 2022 by GMC Publications Ltd, Castle Place, 166 High Street, Lewes,
East Sussex, BN7 1XU
Coordinated by Japan UNI Agency Inc. and LibriSource Inc.
Translator Kevin Wilson
Publisher Jonathan Bailey
Production Director Jim Bulley
Design Manager Robin Shields
Designer Rhiann Bull
Senior Project Editor Virginia Brehaut
Editor Robin Pridy

Reprinted 2024

ISBN 978 1 78494 652 4

Colour origination by GMC Reprographics
Printed and bound in China

To order a book, contact:

GMC Publications Ltd
Castle Place, 166 High Street, Lewes, East
Sussex, BN7 1XU, United Kingdom
Tel: +44 (0)1273 488005
www.gmcbooks.com